THE TWELVE

(Prophecies about ISRAEL and the Day of the Lord)

by

David Hocking

THE TWELVE

Copyright 2016 by HFT Publications
Published by HFT Publications PO Box 3927,
Tustin, CA, 92781 Phone: 1-800-75-BIBLE
Printed in the United States of America

Unless noted otherwise, all Scripture is taken from the
Holy Bible, King James Version, copyright 1982 by
Thomas Nelson, Inc.

ISBN 978-0-939497-43-0

INTRODUCTION

THE TWELVE (Minor Prophets) are critical to our understanding of the future and the Plan of God!

They are described as "Minor" not because their message is brief or not significant; while the "Major Prophets (Isaiah, Jeremiah, Ezekiel, etc.)" contain more words and are bigger in size, these twelve prophetical books are unique in describing the Nation of Israel (both past and future) and its relationship to the coming Day of the LORD.

This book is to be used by students of Israel and Bible prophecy, and is presented in outline form for easier assimilation of the material.

TABLE OF CONTENTS

HOSEA

This is a fascinating story of repentance, forgiveness, and restoration of the Nation of Israel. Because of the mercy of God there is hope! The message of this book is quoted often in the New Testament. We all need to know the wonderful mercy of God Who holds back from us what we really deserve. This book centers its attention upon the need to "RETURN TO THE LORD!"

The problem Bible expositors have with the Minor Prophets is that many of the things that are said in the context of past history did not take place as described. In addition to the very significant phrase "DAY OF THE LORD" there is a frequent usage of the phrase "IN THAT DAY" which often does not apply to the history of their times. Within the historical portions of these 12 books there are prophecies that apply to the future – far beyond the time and understanding of the prophet. There are also many Messianic portions of these twelve books.

It appears that these 12 books focus on Israel as the centerpiece of God's prophetic program. It is used 105 times in these 12 books. The word *"Judah"* is found 63 times. Those who argue that God cancelled His everlasting covenant with Israel because of their sin and disobedience have special problems in trying to interpret the messages in these wonderful books. God's promises to Abraham, Isaac, and Jacob, and their physical descendants did NOT end with the destruction of Jerusalem and the Second Temple in AD 70.

GENERAL OUTLINE OF HOSEA

(197 verses – *Hosea 1:1-14:9*)

1. **THE ILLUSTRATIONS OF UNFAITHULNESS TO GOD!**
   Hosea 1:1-3:5

Key teaching: Their RELATIONSHIP to God was changed!

2. **THE INIQUITIES OF GOD'S PEOPLE!**
   Hosea 4:1-10:15

Key teaching: Their REPENTANCE was lacking!

3. **THE INVITATION of God's love!**
   Hosea 11:1-14:9

Key teaching: Their RESTORATION is promised!

"The word of the LORD that came unto Hosea" – phrase is used 258 times in the Bible!

HISTORICAL BACKGROUND

Hosea was a contemporary of Isaiah the prophet. Uzziah of Judah became king in the 27th year of Jeroboam and he reigned for 52 years, the last sixteen of which included his son Jotham ruling with him because Uzziah was a leper.

Jotham's son, Ahaz, did not do that which was right but *"walked in the way of the kings of Israel"* (II Kings 16:3).

Uzziah and Jeroboam were contemporaries as kings for about 15 years. Jeroboam's son, Zechariah, reigned for just six months, and was assassinated by Shallum who lasted for only one month. He was killed by Menahem who reigned for 10 years and his son Pekahiah ruled for two years, and was assassinated by Pekah, one of his captains, who became king and ruled for 20 years. Pekah began his reign during the last year of Uzziah's life. During Pekah's reign, Tiglath-Pileser of Assyria invaded northern Israel, captured some cities, and took some captives. Pekah was then killed by Hoshea.

Pekah was a contemporary of Jotham who began his reign with his father Uzziah in the second year of Pekah's reign. Ahaz became king of Judah in the 17th year of Pekah's 20 year rule, and ruled for 16 years and paid tribute to Tiglath-Pileser of Assyria to avoid being destroyed by Assyria.

The 12th year of Ahaz's reign is when Shalmaneser, king of Assyria came against Pekah's successor, Hoshea, and carried the northern tribes into captivity to Assyria in 722 BC. Hezekiah became king of Judah in the 3rd year of Hoshea and reigned for 29 years. Hezekiah rebelled against Assyria even though he saw the destruction of the northern kingdom of Israel in the sixth year of his reign.

But, eight years later, Sennacherib, the new king of Assyria came against Hezekiah and because of Hezekiah's prayer to the Lord, the Angel of the Lord defeated the Assyrians in one night, killing 185,000 of them. Sennacherib was killed by his sons back in Assyria and Esarhaddon came to the throne of Assyria.

From Jeroboam's 41 years, it was another 42 years until the destruction of the northern kingdom. During that time the kings of Judah were Uzziah, Jotham, Ahaz, and Hezekiah.

ILLUSTRATIONS OF UNFAITHFULNESS TO GOD
Hosea 1:2-3:5

1. The <u>TAKING</u> of a prostitute for a wife – 1:2-3a

2. The <u>TRIALS</u> of three children – 1:3b-9

3. The <u>TRUTH</u> about Israel's future – 1:10-2:1

4. The <u>TEACHING</u> about God's love – 2:2-3:5

   (1) He will <u>REMOVE</u> His blessing when we are unfaithful to Him! 2:2-13

   (2) He will <u>REACH OUT</u> to us with a door of hope! 2:14-17

(3)   He will <u>REAFFIRM</u> His covenant to us! 2:18

(4)   He will <u>REMIND</u> us of the kind of Lover He is! – 2:19-20

(5)   He will <u>RESTORE</u> His blessing upon us! – 2:21-23

(6)   He will <u>RECEIVE</u> us back when we repent! – 3:1-3

(7)   He will <u>REASSURE</u> us of future blessings! 3:4-5

INIQUITIES OF GOD'S PEOPLE – Hosea 4:1-10:15

1. <u>IGNORANCE</u> of the LORD and His Word – 4:1-5:15

2. <u>INDIFFERENCE</u> to God's Word
   6:1-11a

3. <u>INIQUITY</u> of Ephraim
   7:1-16

4. <u>IDOLATRY</u> of God's people
   8:1-14

5. <u>IMMORALITY</u> of Ephraim
   9:1-17

6. <u>INSINCERITY</u> of the northern
   kingdom of Israel
   10:1-15

The <u>INVITATION</u> of God's love
Hosea 11:1-14:9

1. The <u>CALLING</u> of His people
   11:1-12

2. The <u>CONTROVERSY</u> with Judah –
   12:1-14

3. The <u>CHARACTER</u> of our Lord –
   13:1-16

4. The <u>CALL</u> to return to the Lord –
   14:1-9

RETURN UNTO THE LORD THY GOD!

JOEL

The <u>PICTURE</u> of God's judgment – Joel 1:1-7

"The word of the LORD that came to Joel, the son of Pethuel. Hear this, ye old men, and give ear, all ye inhabitants of the land. Hath this been in your days, or even in the days of your fathers? Tell ye your children of it, and let your children tell their children, and their children another generation. That which the palmer worm hath left hath the locust eaten; and that which the locust hath left hath the cankerworm eaten; and that which the cankerworm hath left hath the caterpillar eaten. Awake, ye drunkards, and weep; and howl, all ye drinkers of wine, because of the new wine; for it is cut off from your mouth. For a nation is come up upon My land, strong, and without number, whose teeth are the teeth of a lion, and he

hath the cheek teeth of a great lion. He hath laid My vine waste, and barked My fig tree; he hath made it clean bare, and cast it away; its branches are made white."

   1. This <u>DESCRIPTION</u> came directly from the Lord – v. 1a

<u>NOTE:</u> The phrase *"the word of the Lord came"* is found 92 times in the Bible; the phrase *"the word of the Lord came unto me"* occurs 46 times of which 37 are in Ezekiel.

   2. The <u>DATING</u> of this message is not easily determined – v. 1b (7th century BC)

There is no knowledge of the prophet or his family; no king is mentioned, or the northern kingdom of Israel which was destroyed in 722 BC. Jerusalem has walls standing (written before 586 BC when Jerusalem and the Temple of

Solomon were destroyed by Babylon. The temple is still standing as well.

   3. The <u>DECLARATION</u> will be given to future generations – vv. 2-3

   4. The <u>DEVASTATION</u> will be overwhelming – v. 4

<u>NOTE:</u> The term *"locusts"* along with the *"palmerworm"* and *"cankerworm"* and *"caterpillar"* comes from four Hebrew words that probably are describing the different kinds of *"locusts."*

The term *gazam* probably refers to the swarm of locusts as they attack the fields; the second word *arbeh* probably refers to the power of these locusts. The third term *yeleq* seems to refer to "young locusts" that have great energy, and are extremely dangerous. The fourth term *hash'* might be a general term for "other locusts." There are at least 10 different Hebrew words that describe the *"locust."*

5. The <u>DRUNKARDS</u> will have nothing to drink – v. 5

6. The <u>DESTRUCTION</u> will come from a strong nation – vv. 6-7

The <u>PLEA</u> for repentance – Joel 1:8-20

"Lament like a virgin girded with sackcloth for the husband of her youth. The meat offering and the drink offering are cut off from the house of the LORD; the priests, the LORD's ministers, mourn. The field is wasted, the land mourneth; for the corn is wasted; the new wine is dried up, the oil languisheth. Be ye ashamed, O ye husbandmen; howl, O ye vinedressers, for the wheat and for the barley, because the harvest of the field is perished. The vine is dried up, and the

fig tree languisheth; the pomegranate tree, the palm tree also, and the apple tree, even all the trees of the field are withered, because joy is withered away from the sons of men. Gird yourselves, and lament, ye priests; howl, ye ministers of the altar; come, lie all night in sackcloth, ye minister of my God; for the meat offering and the drink offering are withholden from the house of your God. Sanctify a fast, call a solemn assembly, gather the elders and all the inhabitants of the land into the house of the LORD, your God, and cry unto the LORD. Alas for the day! For the day of the LORD is at hand, and as a destruction from the Almighty shall it come. Is not the meat cut off before our eyes, yea, joy and gladness from the house of our God? The seed is rotten under their clods, the garners are laid desolate, the barns are broken down; for the corn is withered. How do the beasts groan! The herds of cattle are perplexed, because they have no *pasture; yea, the flocks of sheep are made desolate. O LORD, to Thee will I cry; for the fire hath devoured the pastures of the wilderness, and the flame hath burned all the trees of the field. The beasts of the field cry also unto Thee; for the rivers of waters are dried up, and the fire hath devoured the pastures of the wilderness."*

1. The <u>REACTIONS</u> God wants from His people – vv. 8-14

<u>NOTE:</u> The reaction to this disastrous locust plague brings us the question about God's involvement and our responsibility. Believers handle tragedies and disasters in different ways. For Joel the locust plague was an act of God. Consider the ways that people look at disasters:

(1) It proves God is not involved.

(2)	These disasters are the work of Satan that God allows to exist.

(3)	The disasters are the result of sin in the lives of people.

(4)	God is the cause for reasons and purposes that we cannot understand at the moment.

2. The <u>REASON</u> behind this plea for repentance – vv. 15-20

(1)	The <u>COMING</u> of the Day of the Lord – vv. 15-18

(2)	The <u>CONSEQUENCES</u> of God's judgment – vv. 19-20

The <u>PREPARATION</u> that is needed – Joel 2:1-17

"Blow the trumpet in Zion, and sound an alarm in My holy mountain. Let all the inhabitants of the land tremble; for the day of the LORD cometh, for it is nigh at hand; A day of darkness and of gloominess, a day of clouds and of thick darkness, like the morning spread upon the mountains; a great people and a strong; there hath not been ever the like. Neither shall be any more after it, even to the years of many generations. A fire devoureth before them, and behind them a flame burneth; the land is like the garden of Eden before them, and behind them a desolate wilderness; yea, and nothing shall escape them. The appearance of them is like the appearance of horses; and like horsemen, so shall they run. Like the noise of chariots on the tops of mountains shall they leap, like the noise of a flame of fire that devoureth the stubble, like a strong people set in battle array. Before their face the peoples shall be much pained; all faces

shall gather blackness. They shall run like mighty men; they shall climb the wall like men of war, and they shall march every one on his ways, and they shall not break their ranks. Neither shall one thrust another; they shall walk every one in his path, and when they fall upon the sword, they shall not be wounded. They shall run to and fro in the city; they shall run upon the wall; they shall climb up upon the houses; they shall enter in at the windows like a thief. The earth shall quake before them; the heavens shall tremble; the sun and the moon shall be dark, and the stars shall withdraw their shining: And the LORD shall utter His voice before His army; for His camp is very great; for He is strong Who executeth His word; for the day of the LORD is great and very terrible, and who can abide it? Therefore also, now, saith the LORD, turn even to Me with all your heart, and with fasting, and with weeping, and with mourning;

And rend your heart, and not your garments, and turn unto the LORD, your God: for He is gracious and merciful, slow to anger, and of great kindness, and repenteth Him of the evil. Who knoweth if He will return and repent, and leave a blessing behind Him, even a meal offering and a drink offering unto the LORD, your God? Blow the trumpet in Zion, sanctify a fast, call a solemn assembly. Gather the people, sanctify the congregation, assemble the elders, gather the children, and those that suck the breasts; let the bridegroom go from his chamber, and the bride out of her closet. Let the priests, the minister of the LORD, weep between the porch and the altar, and let them say, Spare Thy people, O LORD, and give not Thine heritage to reproach, that the heathen should rule over them. Wherefore should they say among the people, where is their God?"

<u>NOTE:</u> The word *"trumpet"* is no doubt referring to the Hebrew *"shofar"* which is used 72 times – refers to a ram's horn and was curved without any decoration.

1. The <u>CHARACTER</u> of the coming "Day of the LORD"

It is described as a day of distress (cf. Luke 21:25-26) and a day of darkness. The word *"darkness"* pictures impending judgment. It is also a day of demonism (cf. Revelation 9), devouring, danger, disaster, and destruction.

2. The <u>CALL</u> for repentance – vv. 12-17

"Therefore also, now, saith the LORD, turn even to Me with all your heart, and with fasting, and with weeping, and with mourning; And rend your heart, and not your garments, and turn unto the LORD, your God; for He is gracious and merciful, slow to

anger, and of great kindness, and repenteth Him of the evil. Who knoweth if He will return and repent, and leave a blessing behind Him, even a meat offering and a drink offering unto the LORD, your God? Blow the trumpet in Zion, sanctify a fast, call a solemn assembly. Gather the people, sanctify the congregation, assemble the elders, gather the children, and those that suck the breasts; let the bridegroom go forth from his chamber, and the bride out of her closet. Let the priests, the ministers of the LORD, weep between the porch and the altar, and let them say, Spare Thy people, O LORD, and give not Thine heritage to reproach, that the heathen should rule over them. Wherefore should they say among the people, Where is their God?"

    (1)   The <u>RESPONSE</u> that gives evidence of true repentance – v. 12

(2) The <u>RECOGNITION</u> of the LORD's attributes that draw us to Him! vv. 13-14

(3) The immediate <u>REACTION</u> that is needed – vv. 15-16

(4) The <u>REASONS</u> behind this call to repent – v. 17

The <u>PITY</u> which the LORD will have on His people if they repent! Joel 2:18-27

"Then the LORD was jealous for His land, and pitied His people. Yea, the LORD will answer and say unto His people, Behold, I will send you corn, and wine, and oil, and ye shall be satisfied with them; and I will no more make you a reproach among the heathen, But I will remove far off from you the northern army, and will drive

him into a land barren and desolate, with his face toward the east sea, and his hinder part toward the utmost sea, and his stink shall come up, and his ill savor shall come up, because he hath done great things. Fear not, O land. Be glad and rejoice; for the LORD will do great things. Be not afraid, ye beasts of the field; for the pastures of the wilderness do spring, for the tree beareth her fruit, the fig tree and the vine do yield their strength. Be glad then, ye children of Zion, and rejoice in the LORD, your God; for He hath given you the former rain moderately, and He will cause to come down for you the rain, the former rain and the latter rain in the first month. And the floors shall be full of wheat, and the fats shall overflow with wine and oil. And I will restore to you the years that the locust hath eaten, the cankerworm, and the caterpillar, and the palmer worm, My great army which I sent among you. And ye shall eat in plenty, and be *satisfied, and praise the Name of the LORD, your God, Who hath dealt wondrously with you; and My people shall never be ashamed. And ye shall know that I am in the midst of Israel, and that I am the LORD, your God, and none else; and My people shall never be ashamed."*

1. His <u>ATTITUDE</u> toward His land – v. 18 – *"jealous for His land"*

2. His <u>ANSWER</u> to His people about the northern army that is coming – vv. 19-20

3. His <u>ABILITY</u> should eliminate all fear – vv. 21-22

4. His <u>APPEAL</u> to His people to rejoice – vv. 23-25

5. His <u>ADORATION</u> will come from His people – v. 26

6. His ultimate <u>AIM</u> will be accomplished – v. 27 *"and ye shall know that I am in the midst of Israel, and that I am the LORD your God, and none else, and My people shall never be ashamed."*

The <u>PROMISE</u> of deliverance through the work of the Holy Spirit! Joel 2:28-32
(This is chapter 3 in the Hebrew Bible)

"And it shall come to pass afterward, that I will pour out My Spirit upon all flesh; and your sons and your daughters shall prophesy, your old men shall dream dreams, your young men shall see visions; And, also, upon the servants and upon the handmaids in those days will I pour out My Spirit. And I will show wonders in the heavens and in the earth: blood, and fire, and pillars of smoke. The sun shall be turned into darkness, and the

*moon into blood, before the great and
the terrible day of the LORD come.
And it shall come to pass that
whosoever shall call on the Name of
the LORD shall be delivered; for in
Mount Zion and in Jerusalem shall be
deliverance, as the LORD hath said,
and in the remnant whom the LORD
shall call."*

1. The <u>MEANING</u> of this event – vv.
   28-29 cf. Acts 2:16-21

   (1) It refers to the
        <u>PRESENCE</u> of the Holy
        Spirit in the lives of all
        believers!

   (2) It refers to the <u>POWER</u>
        of the Holy Spirit in
        giving believers
        boldness to witness and
        control over sinful
        attitudes and actions!

2. The <u>MULTITUDE</u> who will receive the Spirit – *"all flesh"*

3. The <u>MARVELS</u> that will occur in the heavens and on the earth – vv. 30-31 – *"wonders"*

4. The <u>MIRACLE</u> of deliverance – v. 32a

5. The <u>MOUNT</u> where this will take place – v. 32b – *"for in mount Zion and in Jerusalem shall be deliverance"*

6. The <u>MOMENT</u> that this will occur – *'and it shall come to pass"*

The <u>PREDICTION</u> of God's final victory over all nations!
Joel 3:1-21

1. The <u>RETURN</u> of the Jewish people will mark the time – v. 1 *"in those days, and in that time"*

2. The <u>REASONS</u> behind the judgment of God are clear – vv. 2-3 *"I will gather all nations"*

3. The <u>RECOMPENSE</u> of God will come to the nations – vv. 4-8 *"Tyre, Zidon, and all the coasts of Palestine* (Philistia)

4. The <u>ROUSING</u> of the nations to battle will be accomplished by the LORD Himself – vv. 9-12 – *"there will I sit to judge all the heathen* (nations) *round about"*

5. The <u>RIPENESS</u> of judgment is based on the greatness of their wickedness – v. 13

6. The <u>REALIZATION</u> that the Day of the LORD has come – vv. 14-15 *"the sun and the moon shall be darkened, and the stars shall withdraw their shining"*

7. The <u>ROARING</u> of the LORD will announce His intervention for His people – v. 16 – *"the LORD will be the hope of His people"*

The **<u>RECOGNITION</u>** of the LORD will be obvious to His people!   Joel 3:17-21

"So shall ye know that I am the LORD, your God, dwelling in Zion, My holy mountain; then shall Jerusalem be holy, and there shall no strangers pass through her any more. And it shall come to pass, in that day, that the mountains shall drop down new wine, and the hills shall flow with milk, and all the rivers of Judah shall flow with waters, and a fountain shall come forth from the house of the LORD, and water the Valley of Shittim. Egypt shall be a desolation, and Edom shall be a desolate wilderness, for the violence against the children of Judah, because they have shed innocent blood in their land. But Judah shall dwell forever, and Jerusalem from generation to generation. For I will cleanse their blood that I have not cleansed; for the LORD dwelleth in Zion."

AMOS

INTRODUCTION to the Book
Amos 1:1-2

We are told that this prophet is from Tekoa, a town situated on the borders of the desert of Judea, about two hours south of Bethlehem. Amos says that he is not a prophet nor the son of one. He was *"an herdsman, and a gatherer of sycamore fruit."*

"The words of Amos, who was among the herdsmen of Tekoa, which he saw in the days of Uzziah, king of Judah, and in the days of Jeroboam, the son of Joash, king of Israel, two years before the earthquake. And he said, The LORD will roar from Zion, and utter His voice from Jerusalem; and the habitations of the shepherds shall mourn, and the top of Carmel shall wither."

The name *"Amos"* is the Hebrew word for *"bearer"* or *"burden."* He was a contemporary of Hosea and his

ministry seems to center in Bethel
(golden calf)

1. The <u>DATE</u> of this prophecy – *"days
of Uzziah (790-740 BC)"* and *"the
days of Jeroboam II (793-753 BC)"*
and *"two years before the
earthquake."*

The *"earthquake"* was probably the
same as the one mentioned by
Zechariah. Josephus connects this
earthquake with the pride of Uzziah
that brought about his leprosy. But that
is impossible. Uzziah survived
Jeroboam II by 26 years, and Jotham,
Uzziah's son, judged Israel after his
father's leprosy, and he was not even
born when Jeroboam died.

2. The <u>DETAILS</u> of his message
Amos 1:3 -2:16

(1)   The <u>PUNISHMENT</u> of
Damascus – 1:3-5

*"Thus saith the LORD: For three
transgressions of Damascus, and for
four, I will not turn away its*

punishment, because they have threshed Gilead with threshing instruments of iron. But I will send a fire into the house of Hazael, which shall devour the palaces of Ben-hadad. I will break also the bar of Damascus, and cut off the inhabitant from the plain of Aven, and him that holdeth the scepter from the house of Eden; and the people of Syria shall go into captivity unto Kir, saith the LORD."

The phrase *"for three transgressions...and for four"* is only used in Amos, referring to six nations that were the enemies of Israel. In six of those judgment passages, we read the LORD saying: *"I will not turn away."* The judgment of the LORD was coming and nothing could stop it!

2. The <u>PUNISHMENT</u> of Gaza Amos 1:6-8

"Thus saith the LORD: For three transgressions of Gaza, and for four, I will not turn away its punishment, because they carried away captive the whole captivity, to deliver them up to

Edom; But I will send a fire on the wall of Gaza, which shall devour its palaces. And I will cut off the inhabitant from Ashdod, and him that holdeth the scepter from Ashkelon, and I will turn Mine hand against Ekron; and the remnant of the Philistines shall perish, saith the Lord GOD."

Gaza means "strong" – there were five Philistine cities in that area: Gaza, Ashdod, Ashkelon, Ekron, and Gath.

3. The <u>PUNISHMENT</u> of Tyre
Amos 1:9-10

"Thus saith the LORD: For three transgressions of Tyre, and for four, I will not turn away its punishment, because they delivered up the whole captivity to Edom, and remembered not the brotherly covenant; But I will send a fire on the wall of Tyre, which shall devour its palaces."

Tyre was known for its maritime exploits and its export of purpose dye. Ezekiel 28 refers to the king of Tyre as the ultimate example of pride, with the references connected to Satan himself.

4. The <u>PUNISHMENT</u> of Edom
   Amos 1:11-12

"Thus saith the LORD: For three transgressions of Edom, and for four, I will not turn away its punishment, because he did pursue his brother with the sword, and did cast off all pity, and his anger did tear perpetually, and he kept his wrath forever; But I will send a fire upon Teman, which shall devour the palaces of Bozrah."

5. The <u>PUNISHMENT</u> of Ammon
   Amos 1:13-15

"Thus saith the LORD: For three transgressions of the children of Ammon, and for four, I will not turn away their punishment, because they have ripped up the women with child in Gilead, that they might enlarge their border; But I will kindle a fire in the wall of Rabbah, and it shall devour its palaces, with shouting in the day of battle, with a tempest in the day of the

whirlwind; and their king shall go into captivity, he and his princes together, saith the LORD."

6. The <u>PUNISHMENT</u> of Moab
Amos 2:1-3

Thus saith the LORD: For three transgressions of Moab, and for four, I will not turn away its punishment, because he burned the bones of the king of Edom into lime; But I will send a fire upon Moab, and it shall devour the palaces of Kerioth; and Moab shall die with tumult, with shouting, and with the sound of the trumpet. And I will cut off the judge from the midst of it, and slay all its princes with him, saith the LORD."

7. The <u>PUNISHMENT</u> of Judah
Amos 2:4-5

"Thus saith the LORD: For three transgressions, and for four, I will not turn away its punishment, because they have despised the law of the LORD, and have not kept His commandments, and their lies caused

them to err, after which their fathers have walked; But I will send a fire upon Judah, and it shall devour the palaces of Jerusalem."

When human opinion substitutes for the Word of God the result is always the same. We start to believe *"the lies"* – and that always starts when our attitude changes toward the Word of God.

The devouring of the palaces of Jerusalem no doubt occurred when Babylon attacked and destroyed the Temple of Solomon and the city (586 BC).

8. The <u>PUNISHMENT</u> of Israel
Amos 2:6-8

"Thus saith the LORD: For three transgressions of Israel, and for four, I will not turn away its punishment, because they sold the righteous for silver, and the poor for a pair of shoes, that pant after the dust of the earth on the head of the poor, and turn aside the way of the meek; and a man and his

father will go in unto the same maid, to profane My holy Name. And they lay themselves down upon clothes laid to pledge by every altar, and they drink the wine of the condemned in the house of their god."

1. The <u>REASONS</u> for God's judgment upon the northern kingdom of Israel

     (1)   INJUSTICE – V. 6
     (2)   INSENSITIVTY – v. 7a
     (3)   IMMORALITY – v. 7b
     (4)   IDOLATRY – v. 8

2. The <u>REMINDER</u> of God's blessings Amos 2:9-11

"Yet destroyed I the Amorite before them, whose height was like the height of the cedars, and he was as strong as the oaks; yet I destroyed his fruit from above, and his roots from beneath. Also I brought you up from the land of Egypt, and led you

forty years through the wilderness, to possess the land of the Amorite. And I raised up of your sons for prophets, and of your young men for Nazirites. Is it not even thus, O ye children of Israel? saith the LORD."

1. God's <u>DESTRUCTION</u> of the Amorites – v. 9

2. God's <u>DELIVERANCE</u> from Egypt – v. 10a

3. Their <u>DEPENDENCY</u> upon God in the wilderness – v. 10b

4. God's <u>DEVELOPMENT</u> of religious leaders – v. 11

The <u>RESULTS</u> they could expect – vv. 12-16

1. Their <u>REFUSAL</u> to accept God's leaders and their messages would bring God's judgment – v. 12

2. The <u>REACTION</u> of the LORD reveals the problem – v. 13

3. Their __RESPONSES__ will not deliver them – vv. 14-16

The __REALIZATION__ that they will not escape the judgment of the LORD – Amos 3:1-15

1. The __PUNISHMENT__ that God will bring – vv. 2-3

2. The __PRINCIPLE__ that is involved – v. 3

3. The __PICTURES__ that teach that judgment is coming – vv. 4-6

4. The __PANIC__ that will come – vv. 7-8

5. The __PROPHECY__ must be given – *"The LORD hath spoken"*

6. The __PUBLISHING__ of what God will do – vv. 9-15

The __REASONS__ for the LORD's coming judgment
Amos 4:1-9:10

1. Their <u>RETURN</u> to the Lord did not happen – 4:1-13

2. Their <u>REFUSAL</u> to seek the Lord was obvious – 5:1-27

3. The <u>RELIANCE</u> upon themselves would prove to be a disaster – 6:1-14

4. Their <u>RESISTANCE</u> to the message of the prophet would bring the judgment of the LORD upon them – 7:1-17

5. Their <u>RESPECT</u> for the poor and needy was neglected and abused – 8:1-14

6. Their <u>REBELLION</u> would not hide them from the LORD – 9:1-10

The <u>RESTORATION</u> of Israel
Amos 9:11-15

"In that day will I raise up the tabernacle of David that is fallen, and close up the breaches of it; and I will raise up his ruins, and I will

build it as in the days of old, that they may possess the remnant of Edom, and of all the heathen, which are called by My Name, saith the LORD Who doeth this. Behold the days come, saith the LORD, that the plowman shall overtake the reaper, and the treader of grapes him that soweth seed; and the mountains shall drop sweet wine, and all the hills shall melt. And I will bring again the captivity of My people of Israel, and they shall build the waste cities, and inhabit them; and they shall plant vineyards, and drink their wine; they shall also make gardens, and eat the fruit of them. And I will plant them upon their land, and they shall no more be pulled up out of their land which I have given them, saith the LORD, thy God."

1. The <u>PLACE</u> of worship will be rebuilt – 9:11

2. The <u>POSSESSION</u> of the nations will be fulfilled – 9:12

3. Agricultural __PRODUCTIVITY__ will be amazing – v. 13

4. The Jewish __PEOPLE__ will return from captivity – v. 14

5. The __PROMISE__ of God will never allow them to be uprooted from their land – v. 15

In spite of their sin and unbelief, God will be faithful to His promises!

OBADIAH
Obadiah 1-21

INTRODUCTION – Obadiah 1:1-2

"The vision of Obadiah. Thus saith the Lord GOD concerning Edom: We have heard a rumor from the LORD, and an ambassador is sent among the heathen, Arise, and let us rise up against her in battle. Behold, I have made thee small among the heathen; thou art greatly despised."

The name *"Obadiah"* means *"a servant of the LORD."* Viewpoints about his identity include I Kings 18:3-4 – *"the governor of his house* (Ahab)*"* – the one who hid 100 prophets in caves and fed them. Others go to II Chronicles 17:7-9 and see him as one of the *"princes"* of Jehoshaphat sent to teach in the cities of Judah; Others go to II Chronicles 34:12 and see him as one of the *"overseers"* that Josiah appointed to repair the temple.

The prophecy of the <u>DESTRUCTION</u> of Edom – vv. 3-14

1. They were <u>DECEIVED!</u> v. 3

"The pride of thine heart hath deceived thee, thou who dwellest in the clefts of the rock, whose habitation is high, who saith in his heart, Who shall bring me down to the ground?

It seemed in ancient times, that this piece of land known as Edom was unconquerable. Edom was located on the main trade route known as "the King's Highway" which runs from Egypt to Iraq – Cairo to Baghdad.

2. They would be <u>DEFEATED!</u> v. 4

"Though thou exalt thyself like the eagle, and though thou set thy nest among the stars, from there will I bring thee down, saith the LORD."

3. They were <u>DISALLUSIONED</u> by their confederacy with others – vv. 5-7

"If thieves came to thee, if robbers by night (how art thou cut off!) would they not have stolen till they had enough? If the grape gatherers came to thee, would they not leave some grapes? How are the things of Esau searched out! How are his hidden things sought up! All the men of thy confederacy have brought thee even to the border; the men that were at peace with thee have deceived thee, and prevailed against thee; they that eat thy bread have laid a wound under thee; there is none understanding in him."

4. They were <u>DISMAYED!</u> vv. 8-9

"Shall I not in that day, saith the LORD, even destroy the wise men out of Edom, and understanding out of the mount of Esau? And thy mighty men, O Teman, shall be dismayed, to the end that every one of the mount of Esau may be cut off by slaughter."

5. They were __DISOBEDIENT__ in their attitudes and actions toward Israel – vv. 10-14

    (1)   They __RESPONDED__ happily over their captivity!

    (2)   They __REJOICED__ when Judah was destroyed!

    (3)   They __REACTED__ with pride when Israel was in distress!

    (4)   They __ROBBED__ them in the day of their calamity!

    (5)   They __REFUSED__ to help them when they were afflicted!

    (6)   They __RESISTED__ their attempts to escape!

    (7)   They __RETURNED__ them to those who attacked them!

The prophecy of the __DAY__ of the LORD Obadiah 15-16

"For the day of the LORD is near upon all the heathen. As thou hast done, it shall be done unto thee; thy reward shall return upon thine own head. For as ye have drunk upon My holy mountain, so shall all the heathen drink continually; yea, they shall drink, and they shall swallow down, and they shall be as though they had not been."

1. The <u>EXTENT</u> to which this Day of the LORD will affect the world!

2. The <u>EXECUTION</u> of God's revenge!

3. The <u>EFFECT</u> of this judgment!

The prophecy of the <u>DELIVERANCE</u> upon Mount Zion – Obadiah 17-21

1. The <u>PLACE</u> – Mount Zion – v. 17

2. The <u>PROPHECY</u> of spiritual blessing – v. 17a

3. The **<u>PREDICTION</u>** of physical blessings – vv. 17b-20

4. The **<u>PROMISE</u>** of the Messianic kingdom – v. 21

JONAH
Jonah 1:1-4:11

In only 48 verses, there is just one prophetic announcement (Jonah 3:4): *"Yet forty days, and Nineveh shall be overthrown!"* (just five Hebrew words!)

Theme of the Book: GOD'S LOVE FOR ALL NATIONS!

The Book of Jonah is read on the Day of Atonement (Yom Kippur) because of its emphasis on repentance.

GOD'S <u>CALL</u> — Jonah 1:1-16

1. The LORD <u>SPEAKS</u> His word and will — 1:1-2

"Now the word of the LORD came unto Jonah, the son of Amittai, saying, Arise, go to Nineveh, that great city, and cry against it; for their wickedness is come up before Me."

Ancient Nineveh had a wall around it over 100 feet high. Three chariots could race abreast on top of it. The wall had 1500 towers that stood 100 feet higher than the wall! The city covered a land area of 350 square miles.

After Nineveh was destroyed in 612 BC, it was never rebuilt.

Excavations that began in 1840 AD uncovered over 25,000 tablets from the library of Ashurbanipal.

2. The LORD <u>SEES</u> His servant trying to run away – 1:3

"But Jonah rose up to flee unto Tarshish from the presence of the LORD, and went down to Joppa, and he found a ship going to Tarshish; so he paid the fare, and went down into it, to go with them unto Tarshish from the presence of the LORD."

3. The LORD <u>SENDS</u> a storm to call His servant back to His Word and will – 1:4-15

    (1)   The **<u>REACTION</u>** of the
            mariners

    (2)   The **<u>RESPONSE</u>** of Jonah
            "for I know that for my sake
            this great tempest is upon
            you"

4. The LORD **<u>SAVES</u>** the mariners
and illustrates His love for all
people – v. 16

    (1)   They **<u>DISPLAYED</u>** true
            repentance!

    (2)   They **<u>DEMONSTRATED</u>** their
            faith!

    (3)   They **<u>DECIDED</u>** to follow the
            LORD from now on!

GOD'S <u>CONTROL</u>
Jonah 1:17-2:10

1. The Lord <u>PREPARED</u> a great fish – v. 17

"Now the LORD had prepared a great fish to swallow up Jonah. And Jonah was in the belly of the fish three days and three nights."

2. Jonah <u>PRAYED</u> a great prayer – 2:1-9

    (1)   He <u>RELIED</u> upon the LORD to deliver him – v. 2a

"And said, I cried by reason of mine affliction unto the LORD, and He heard me; out of the belly of hell (Sheol) cried I, and Thou heardest my voice."

    (2)   He <u>REFERRED</u> to the fact that God hears our prayers when we cry unto Him – v. 2b *"Thou heardest my voice"*

    (3)   He <u>REALIZED</u> that God was behind his difficult circumstances – v. 3

"For Thou hadst cast me into the deep, in the midst of the seas, and the floods

*compassed me about; all Thy billows
and Thy waves passed over me."*

      (4)   He <u>RECOGNIZED</u> that only
               the LORD could rescue him
               from his situation – vv. 4-6

*"Then I said, I am cast out of Thy sight;
yet I will look again toward Thine holy
temple. The waters compassed me
about, even to the soul; the depth
closed me round about, the weeds were
wrapped about my head. I went down
to the bottoms of the mountains; the
earth, with its bars, was about me
forever; yet hast Thou brought up my
life from corruption, O LORD, my
God."*

        (1)   He <u>PROMISED</u> to look
                  again to the LORD –
                  v. 4

        (2)   He <u>PRAISED</u> the LORD
                  for saving him from
                  certain death – vv. 5-6

  5. He <u>REMEMBERED</u> the LORD in
     his distress – v. 7

"When my soul fainted within me, I remembered the LORD; and my prayer came in unto Thee, into Thine holy temple."

    6. He <u>RESPONDED</u> with thanksgiving – vv. 8-9a

"They that observe lying vanities forsake their own mercy. But I will sacrifice unto Thee with the voice of thanksgiving"

    7. He <u>RETURNED</u> to the will of God – v. 9b

"I will pay that that I have vowed. Salvation is of the LORD."

3. The LORD <u>PLANNED</u> a great deliverance – v. 10

"And the LORD spoke unto the fish, and it vomited out Jonah upon the dry land."

GOD'S <u>COMPASSION</u>
Jonah 3:1-10

1. God's <u>PATIENCE</u> with His servant is encouraging to all who need a second chance! v. 1

"And the word of the LORD came unto Jonah the second time"

2. God's <u>PRIORITY</u> for His servant is dependent upon obedience – v. 2

"Arise, go unto Nineveh, that great city, according to the word of the LORD. Now Nineveh was an exceedingly great city of three days' journey."

3. Jonah's <u>PREACHING</u> to Nineveh was a message of coming judgment – vv. 3-4

"Therefore now, O LORD, take, I beseech Thee, my life from me; for it is better for me to die than to live. Then

said the LORD, Doest thou well to be angry?"

4. Nineveh's <u>PROOF</u> of repentance – vv. 5-9

"So the people of Nineveh believed God, and proclaimed a fast, and put on sackcloth, from the greatest of them even to the least of them. For word came unto the king of Nineveh, and he arose from his throne, and he laid his robe from him, and covered himself with sackcloth, and sat in ashes." And he caused it to be proclaimed and published through Nineveh by the decree of the king and his nobles, saying, Let neither man nor beast, herd nor flock, taste anything; let them not feed, nor drink water. But let man and beast be covered with sackcloth, and cry mightily unto God; yea, let them turn every one from his evil way, and from the violence that is in their hands. Who can tell if God will turn and repent, and turn away from His fierce anger, that we perish not?"

5. God's <u>PLAN</u> to destroy Nineveh
was changed – v. 10

*"And God saw their works, that they
turned from their evil way; and God
repented of the evil that He had said
that He would do unto them, and He
did it not."*

GOD'S <u>CONCERN</u>
Jonah 4:1-11

1. The <u>ANGER</u> of Jonah was quite
revealing – vv. 1-3

*"But it displeased Jonah exceedingly,
and he was very angry. And he prayed
unto the LORD, and said, I pray thee, O
LORD, was not this my saying, when I
was yet in my country? Therefore, I
fled before unto Tarshish; for I knew
that Thou art a gracious God, and
merciful, slow to anger, and of great
kindness, and repentest Thee of the
evil. Therefore now, O LORD, take, I
beseech Thee, my life from me; for it is
better for me to die than to live.*

(1) He **INFORMS** the LORD of what the LORD already knows!

(2) He **INDICATES** that the LORD's character toward the nations was the real reason he tried to run away in the first place!

(3) He **IMPLIES** that death is better than life under these circumstances!

2. The **ANSWER** of the LORD reveals the problem in Jonah's heart – v. 4

"Then said the LORD, Doest thou well to be angry?"

3. The **ATTITUDE** of Jonah is clearly exposed by the plant – vv. 5-8

"So Jonah went out of the city, and sat on the east side of the city, and there made a booth for himself, and sat under it in the shadow, till he might see what would become of the city. And

the LORD God prepared a gourd, and made it to come up over Jonah, that it might be a shadow over his head, to deliver him from his grief. So Jonah was exceedingly glad of the gourd. But God prepared a worm when the morning rose the next day, and it smote the gourd that it withered. And it came to pass, when the sun did rise, that God prepared a vehement east wind; and the sun beat upon the head of Jonah, that he fainted, and wished in himself to die, and said, It is better for me to die than to live."

4. The <u>APPLICATION</u> for Jonah and for all who read and study this amazing story – vv. 9-11

"And God said to Jonah, Doest thou well to be angry for the gourd? And he said, I do well to be angry, even unto death. Then said the LORD, Thou hast had pity on the gourd, for which thou hast not labored, neither madest it grow; which came up in a night, and perished in a night. And should not I spare Nineveh, that great city, in which are more than sixscore thousand

persons that cannot discern between their right hand and their left hand; and also much cattle?"

MICAH
Micah 1:1-7:20

INTRODUCTION TO THE BOOK
Micah 1:1

"The word of the LORD that came to Micah, the Morasthite, in the days of Jotham, Ahaz, and Hezekiah, kings of Judah, which he saw concerning Samaria and Jerusalem."

1. The <u>SOURCE</u> of this prophecy –
    "the word of the LORD"

2. The <u>SEER</u> who received this message from the LORD – *"Micah the Morasthite"* – the word *"Micah"* comes from *"Micaiahu"* - Who is like the LORD"

Micah 7:18-20 – *"Who is a God like unto Thee, Who pardoneth iniquity, and passeth by the transgression of the remnant of His heritage? He retaineth not His anger forever, because He delighteth in mercy. He will turn again; He will have compassion upon us; He will subdue our iniquities; and Thou wilt cast all their sins into the depths of the sea. Thou wilt perform the truth to Jacob, and the mercy to Abraham, which Thou hast sworn unto our fathers from the days of old."*

His village was Moresheth Gath – Eusebius and Jerome both said that it was "a little village – east of Eleutheropolis (about 25 miles southwest of Jerusalem – near the Philistine city of Gath and also near Lachish) – it was supposedly not only his birthplace, but his burial place – a church was built there in Jerome's day.

3. The <u>SOVEREIGNS</u> of Judah who heard these awesome words of coming judgment – *"in the days of Jotham, Ahaz, and Hezekiah, kings of Judah"*

4. The <u>SUBJECT</u> of this prophecy – *"which he saw concerning Samaria and Jerusalem."*

The **COMING** of judgment –
Micah 1:2-3:12

RESPOND to its urgency!
Micah 1:2-4

"Hear, all ye peoples; hearken, O earth, and all that is in it; and let the Lord GOD be witness against you, the Lord from His holy temple. For, behold, the LORD cometh forth out of His place, and will come down, and tread upon the high places of the earth. And the mountains shall be melten under Him, and the valleys shall be cleft, like wax before the fire, and like the waters that are poured down a steep place."

RECOGNIZE the cause!
Micah 1:5

"For the transgression of Jacob is all this, and for the sins of the house of Israel. What is the transgression of Jacob? Is it not Samaria? And what are the high places of Judah? Are they not Jerusalem?

REMEMBER what Samaria is facing!

Micah 1:6-8 – *"Therefore, I will make Samaria like an heap of the field, and like plantings of a vineyard; and I will pour down its stones into the valley, and I will discover the foundations of it. And all the graven images of it shall be beaten to pieces, and all its rewards shall be burned with the fire, and all its idols will I lay desolate; for she gathered it of the hire of an harlot, and they shall return to the hire of an harlot. Therefore, I will wail and howl. I will go stripped and naked; I will make a wailing like the dragons, and mourning like the owls."*

It was Sargon II of Assyria that carried out this devastation of Samaria in 722 BC.

REALIZE what will happen to Judah – Micah 1:9-16

"For her wound is incurable; for it is come unto Judah; he is come unto the gate of My people, even to Jerusalem. Declare it not at Gath, weep not at all; in the house of Aphrah, roll thyself in the dust. Pass away, thou inhabitant of Shaphir, having thy shame naked; the inhabitant of Zaanan came not forth; in the mourning of Bethezel he shall receive of you his standing. For the inhabitant of Maroth waited carefully for good, but evil came down from the LORD unto the gate of Jerusalem. O thou inhabitant of Lachish, bind the chariot to the swift beast; she is the beginning of sin to the daughter of Zion; for the transgressions of Israel were found in thee. Therefore shalt thou give presents to Moresheth-Gath; the houses of Achzib shall be a lie to the kings of Israel. Yet will I bring an heir unto thee, O inhabitant of Mareshah; he shall come unto Adullam, the glory of Israel. Make thee bald, and poll thee for thy delicate children; enlarge thy baldness as the eagle; for they are gone into captivity from thee."

1. Its <u>CORRUPTION</u> came from Samaria!

2. Its <u>CITIES</u> will be destroyed by Assyria (46 of them – only Jerusalem was spared by Divine intervention – it occurred in 701 BC)

3. Its <u>CAPTIVITY</u> will be extensive!

<u>REMOVE</u> the wickedness!
Micah 2:1-13

1. The <u>PRACTICE</u> of evil which characterizes them – vv. 1-2

"Woe to them that devise iniquity, and work evil upon their beds! When the morning is light, they practice it, because it is in the power of their hand. And they covet fields, and take them by violence, and houses, and take them away; so they oppress a man and his house, even a man and his heritage."

2. The <u>PARABLE</u> that describes what God will do – vv. 3-6

"Therefore, thus saith the LORD: Behold, against this family do I devise an evil, from which ye shall not remove your necks, neither shall ye go haughtily; for this time is evil. In that day shall one take up a parable against you, and lament with a doleful lamentation, and say, We are utterly spoiled; he hath changed the portion of My people. How hath he removed it from Me! Turning away, he hath divided our fields. Therefore, thou shalt have none that shall cast a cord by lot in the congregation of the LORD. Prophesy not, say they to them that prophesy; they shall not prophesy to them, that they shall not take shame."

The **PEOPLE** that have forgotten the word and works of the LORD – v. 7

"O thou that art named the house of Jacob, is the Spirit of the LORD straitened? Are these His doings? Do not My words do good to him that walketh uprightly?

The **POLLUTION** that has resulted – vv. 8-11

"Even of late My people are risen up as an enemy; ye pull off the robe with the garment from them that pass by securely, as men averse from war. The women of My people have ye cast out from their pleasant houses; from their children have ye taken away My glory forever. Arise, and depart; for this is not your rest; because it is polluted, it shall destroy you, even with a sore destruction. If a man, walking in the spirit and falsehood, do lie, saying, I will prophesy unto thee of wine and of strong drink; he shall even be the prophet of this people."

The **PLANS** of the Lord will not be changed! vv. 12-13

"I will surely assemble, O Jacob, all of thee; I will surely gather the remnant of Israel; I will put them together like the sheep of Bozrah, like the flock in the midst of their fold; they shall make great noise by reason of the multitude of men. The breaker is come up before them; they have broken up, and have passed through the gate, and are gone

out by it; and their king shall pass before them, and the LORD at the head of them."

RESIST the leadership!
Micah 3:1-12

   1. The **PRINCES** are devoid of sound judgment – vv. 1-4

"And I said, Hear, I pray you, O heads of Jacob, and ye princes of the house of Israel, Is it not for you to know judgment? Who hate the good, and love the evil; who pluck off their skin from them, and their flesh from their bones; who also eat the flesh of My people, and flay their skin from them; and they break their bones, and chop them in pieces, as for the pot, and like flesh within the caldron. Then shall they cry unto the LORD, but He will not hear them; He will even hide His face from them at that time, as they have behaved themselves ill in their doings."

   2. The **PROPHETS** are without a vision from God – vv. 5-7

"Thus saith the LORD concerning the prophets that make My people err, that bite with their teeth, and cry, Peace; and he that putteth not into their mouths, they even prepare war against him: Therefore night shall be unto you, that ye shall not have a vision; and it shall be dark unto you, that ye shall not divine; and the sun shall go down over the prophets, and the day shall be dark over them. Then shall the seers be ashamed, and the diviners confounded; yea, they shall all cover their lips; for there is no answer from God."

The **<u>PROPHET</u>** of God speaks only what God tells him to say – vv. 8-12

"But truly I am full of power by the Spirit of the LORD, and of judgment, and of might, to declare unto Jacob his transgression, and to Israel his sin. Hear this, I pray you, ye heads of the house of Jacob, and princes of the house of Israel, that abhor judgment, and pervert all equity. They build up Zion with blood and Jerusalem with iniquity. Her heads judge for reward

and her priests teach for hire and her prophets divine for money; yet will they lean upon the LORD, and say, Is not the LORD among us? None evil can come upon us. Therefore shall Zion for your sake be plowed as a field, and Jerusalem shall become heaps and the mountain of the house as the high places of the forest."

The **COMFORT** of the last days – Micah 4:1-5:15

THE COMFORT OF A **SPECIAL PLACE** – 4:1-7

1. The **MEANING** of the term *"last days"* – v. 1

"But in the last days it shall come to pass, that the mountain of the house of the LORD shall be established in the top of the mountains, and it shall be exalted above the hills, and people shall flow unto it."

2. The <u>MOUNTAIN</u> of the Lord's house – v. 1b

3. The <u>MULTITUDES</u> who will come there – v. 2a – *"many nations shall come"*

Psalm 66:4 – *"All the earth shall worship Thee"*

Zechariah 14:16 – *"shall go up from year to year to worship the King, the LORD of hosts, and to keep the feast of tabernacles."*

4. The <u>MOTIVE</u> for going to this house – v. 2b – *"He will teach us of His ways, and we will walk in His paths; for the law shall go forth from Zion, and the word of the LORD from Jerusalem."*

5. The <u>MARVEL</u> of no more war – v. 3 – *"And He shall judge among many people, and rebuke strong nations afar off; and they shall beat their swords into plowshares, and their spears into pruning hooks; nation shall not*

lift up a sword against nation, neither shall they learn war any more."

6. The <u>MOUTH</u> of the LORD – v. 4 – *"But they shall sit every man under his vine and under his fig tree, and none shall make them afraid; for the mouth of the LORD of hosts hath spoken it."*

7. The <u>MIRACLE</u> of a changed people – vv. 5-7a – *"For all people will walk every one in the name of his god, and we will walk in the Name of the LORD, our God forever and ever. In that day, saith the LORD, will I assemble her that halteth, and I will gather her that is driven out, and her that I have afflicted; And I will make her that halted a remnant, and her that was cast far off a strong nation"*

8. The <u>MAJESTY</u> of the coming kingdom – v. 7b – *"and the LORD shall reign over them in Mount Zion from henceforth, even forever."*

(1)   The **PRESENCE** of the Lord Himself is guaranteed – *"and the Lord shall reign over them"*

(2)   The **PLACE** where He will reign – *"Mount Zion"*

(3)   The **PROMISE** of His reign will continue forever – *"even forever"*

THE COMFORT OF A **STRONG PERSON** – 4:8-5:3

1. Seen in the **COMING** of the kingdom He will bring – v. 8

"And thou, O tower of the flock, the stronghold of the daughter of Zion, unto thee shall it come, even the first dominion; the kingdom shall come to the daughter of Jerusalem."

2. Seen in the **CRY** He will hear – vv. 9-10 – *"as a woman in travail"*

79

"Now why dost thou cry out aloud? Is there no king in thee? Is thy counselor perished? For pangs have taken thee, like a woman in travail. Be in pain, and labor to bring forth, O daughter of Zion, like a woman in travail; for now shalt thou go forth out of the city, and thou shalt dwell in the field, and thou shalt go even to Babylon; there shalt thou be delivered; there the LORD shall redeem thee from the hand of thine enemies."

    3. Seen in the <u>COUNSEL</u> which will gather His people – vv. 11-12

"Now also many nations are gathered against thee, that say, Let her be defiled, and let our eye look upon Zion. But they know not the thoughts of the LORD, neither understand they His counsel; for He shall gather them as the sheaves into the floor."

    4. Seen in the <u>CONSECRATION</u> of their victory to the LORD – v. 13

"Arise and thresh, O daughter of Zion; for I will make thine horn iron, and I

will make thy hoofs brass; and thou shalt beat in pieces many peoples; and I will consecrate their gain unto the LORD, and their substance unto the Lord of the whole earth.”

5. Seen in the <u>CONQUEROR</u> that shall come – 5:1-3

“Now gather thyself in troops, O daughter of troops; he hath laid siege against us; they shall smite the Judge of Israel with a rod upon the check. But thou, Bethlehem Ephrathah, though thou be little among the thousands of Judah, yet out of thee shall He come forth unto Me that is to be Ruler in Israel, Whose goings forth have been from of old, from everlasting. Therefore will He give them up, until the time that she who travaileth hath brought forth; then the remnant of his brethren shall return unto the children of Israel.”

<u>NOTE:</u> Micah 5:1 is the last verse in chapter 4 in the Hebrew Bible.

The <u>COMFORT</u> of a <u>SPECIAL PLACE</u>
Micah 4:1-7

The <u>COMFORT</u> of a <u>STRONG PERSON</u>
Micah 4:8-5:3

The <u>COMFORT</u> of a <u>SOVEREIGN PUNISHMENT</u> Micah 5:4-15

1. The <u>RECOGNITION</u> of the Messiah's greatness will be known in it – v. 4

"And He shall stand and feed in the strength of the LORD, in the majesty of the Name of the LORD, His God; and they shall abide; for now shall He be great unto the ends of the earth."

2. The <u>REALITY</u> of the Messiah's rule will be obvious – v. 5

"And this Man shall be the peace, when the Assyrian shall come into our land; and when he shall tread in our palaces, then shall we raise against him seven shepherds, and eight principal men."

3. The <u>REMNANT</u> of Jacob will exercise the punishment of the Messiah upon all nations – vv. 6-9

"And they shall waste the land of Assyria with the sword, and the land of Nimrod in the entrances of it; thus shall He deliver us from the Assyrian, when he cometh into our land, and when he treadeth within our borders. And the remnant of Jacob shall be in the midst of many people like dew from the LORD, like the showers upon the grass, that tarrieth not for man nor waiteth for the sons of men. And the remnant of Jacob shall be among the Gentiles in the midst of many people, like a lion among the beasts of the forest, like a young lion among the flocks of sheep, who, if he go through, both treadeth down, and teareth in pieces, and none can deliver. Thine hand shall be lifted up upon thine adversaries, and all thine enemies shall be cut off."

4. The <u>REMOVAL</u> of all that Israel trusted and worshipped will take place – vv. 10-14

"And it shall come to pass in that day, saith the LORD, that I will cut off thy horses out of the midst of thee, and I will destroy thy chariots; And I will cut off the cities of thy land, and throw down all thy strongholds; And I will cut off witchcrafts out of thine hand, and thou shalt have no more soothsayers; Thy graven images also will I cut off, and thy standing images out of the midst of thee; and thou shalt no more worship the work of thine hands. And I will pluck up thine groves out of the midst of thee; so will I destroy thy cities."

5. The <u>REVENGE</u> of the Messiah will come upon the nations – v. 15

"And I will execute vengeance in anger and fury upon the heathen, such as they have not heard."

The **CONTROVERSY** of the LORD – Micah 6:1-7:17

1. The **RESPONSE** of the LORD to hear the controversy He has with His people

Micah 6:1-3 – *"Hear now what the LORD saith: Arise, contend before the mountains, and let the hills hear thy voice. Hear ye, O mountains, the LORD's controversy, and ye strong foundations of the earth; for the LORD hath a controversy with His people, and He will plead with Israel. O My people, what have I done unto thee? And wherein have I wearied thee? Testify against Me."*

2. The **REMINDER** of what the LORD has done for His people – vv. 4-5

"For I brought thee up out of the land of Egypt, and redeemed thee out of the house of servants; and I sent before thee Moses, Aaron, and Miriam. O My people, remember now what Balak, king of Moab consulted, and what

Balaam, the son of Beor, answered him from Shittim unto Gilgal, that ye may know the righteousness of the LORD."

3. The <u>REQUIREMENTS</u> of the LORD in worship and sacrifice – vv.6-8

"Wherewith shall I come before the LORD, and bow myself before the High God? Shall I come before Him with burnt offerings, with calves of a year old? Will the LORD be pleased with thousands of rams, or with ten thousands of rivers of oil? Shall I give my first-born for my transgression, the fruit of my body for the sin of my soul? He hath shown thee, O man, what is good; and what doth the LORD require of thee, but to do justly, and to love mercy, and to walk humbly with thy God?"

4. The <u>REASONS</u> why the LORD cries out to them – vv. 9-12

"The LORD's voice crieth unto the city, and the man of wisdom shall see Thy Name; hear ye the rod, and who hath appointed it. Are there yet the

treasures of wickedness in the house of
the wicked, and the scant measure that
is abominable? Shall I count them
pure with the wicked balances, and
with the bag of deceitful weights? For
the rich men are full of violence, and
the inhabitants have spoken lies, and
their tongues is deceitful in their
mouth."

  5. The **RESULTS** which He will cause
     because they do not repent – vv.
     13-15

"Therefore also will I make thee sick in
smiting thee, in making thee desolate
because of thy sins. Thou shalt eat, but
not be satisfied; and thy casting down
shall be in the midst of thee; and thou
shalt take hold, but shall not deliver;
and that which thou deliverest will I
give up to the sword. Thou shalt sow,
but thou shalt not reap; thou shalt
tread the olives, but thou shalt not
anoint thyself with oil; and sweet wine,
but shalt not drink wine.

  6. The **REPROACH** which they will
     bear – v. 16

"For the statutes of Omri are kept, and all the works of the house of Ahab, and ye walk in their counsels, that I should make thee a desolation, and your inhabitants an hissing; therefore, ye shall bear the reproach of My people."

      7. **The <u>REALIZATION</u> that our only hope is in the LORD – Micah 7:1-7**

"Woe is me! For I am as when they have gathered the summer fruits, as the grape gleanings of the vintage; there is no cluster to eat; my soul desired the first-ripe fruit. The good man is perished out of the earth, and there is none upright among men; they all lie in wait for blood; they hunt every man his brother with a net. That they may do evil with both hands earnestly, the prince asketh, and the judge asketh for a reward; and the great man, he uttereth his mischievous desire; so they wrap it up. The best of them is like a brier; the most upright is sharper than a thorn hedge; the day of thy watchmen and thy visitation

cometh; now shall be their perplexity. Trust not in a friend, put not confidence in a guide; keep the doors of thy mouth from her that lieth in thy bosom. For the son dishonoreth the father, the daughter riseth up against her mother, the daughter-in-law against her mother-in-law; a man's enemies are the men of his own house. Therefore, I will look unto the LORD; I will wait for the God of my salvation; my God will hear me."

8. The <u>REJOICING</u> of Israel's enemies will one day be gone – Micah 7:8-13

"Rejoice not against me, O mine enemy; when I fall, I shall arise; when I sit in darkness, the LORD shall be a light unto me. I will bear the indignation of the LORD, because I have sinned against Him, until He plead my cause, and execute judgment for me; He will bring me forth to the light, and I shall behold His righteousness. Then she that is mine enemy shall see it, and shame shall cover her who said unto me, Where is

the LORD, thy God? Mine eyes shall behold her; now shall she be trodden down like the mire of the streets. In the day that thy walls are to be built, in that day shall the decree be far removed. In that day also he shall come even to thee from Assyria, and from the fortified cities, and from the fortress even to the river, and from sea to sea, and from mountain to mountain. Notwithstanding, the land shall be desolate because of them that dwell in it, for the fruit of their doings.*

9. The <u>RESTORATION</u> of God's people is coming – vv. 14-17

"Feed thy people with thy rod, the flock of thine heritage, who dwell solitarily in the wood, in the midst of Carmel; let them feed in Bashan and Gilead, as in the days of old. According to the days of thy coming out of the land of Egypt will I show unto him marvelous things. The nations shall see and be confounded at all their might; they shall lay their hand upon their mouth; their ears shall be deaf. They shall lick

the dust like a serpent; they shall move out of their holes like worms of the earth; they shall be afraid of the LORD, our God, and shall fear because of thee."

The **<u>COMPASSION</u>** of the LORD – Micah 7:18-20

"Who is a God like unto Thee, Who pardoneth iniquity, and passeth by the transgression of the remnant of His heritage? He retaineth not His anger forever, because He delighteth in mercy. He will turn again; He will have compassion upon us; He will subdue our iniquities; and Thou wilt cast all their sins into the depths of the sea. Thou wilt perform the truth to Jacob, and the mercy to Abraham, which Thou hast sworn unto our fathers from the days of old."

NAHUM
Nahum 1:1-3:19

INTRODUCTION –Nahum 1:1

"The burden of Nineveh. The book of the vision of Nahum, the El'koshite."

1. The <u>MEANING</u> of his name – *"comfort"* (the city of Capernaum means "the village of Nahum)

2. The <u>MESSAGE</u> about Nineveh *"the burden of Nineveh"*

Nineveh was conquered and destroyed in 612 BC, so this book was written before that time. It would appear as well that the book was written after 663 BC because the prophet compares the destruction of Nineveh with the destruction of No-Amon or Thebes in Egypt – that was carried out by Ashurbanipal (a very violent ruler who bragged about his atrocities).

Nahum's message refers to the revenge of God. Nineveh was the capital of the Assyrian Empire, which was located on the Tigris River, According to the Bible, it was Nimrod (Genesis 10:8-12) who founded Nineveh.

Nahum was a contemporary of Isaiah and Micah.

THE <u>REVENGE</u> OF THE LORD – Nahum 1:2-8

"God is jealous, and the LORD revengeth; the LORD revengeth, and is furious; the LORD will take vengeance on His adversaries, and He reserveth wrath for His enemies. The LORD is slow to anger, and great in power, and will not at all acquit the wicked; the LORD hath His way in the whirlwind and in the storm, and the clouds are the dust of His feet. He rebuketh the sea, and maketh it dry, and drieth up all the rivers; Bashan languisheth, and Carmel; and the flower of Lebanon languisheth. The mountains quake before Him, and the hills melt, and the earth is burned at His presence, yea,

the world, and all that dwell in it. Who can stand before His indignation? And who can abide in the fierceness of His anger? His fury is poured out like fire, and the rocks are thrown down by Him. The LORD is good, a stronghold in the day of trouble, and He knoweth those who trust in Him. But with an overrunning flood He will make an utter end of the place, and darkness shall pursue His enemies."

Romans 12:19 – *"Vengeance if Mine; I will repay, saith the Lord."*

Deuteronomy 32:35 – *"To Me belongeth vengeance, and recompence."*

Isaiah 34:8 – *"For it is the day of the LORD's vengeance, and the year of recompences for the controversy of Zion."*

Isaiah 63:4 – *"For the day of vengeance is in Mine heart."*

1. The LORD's <u>PATIENCE</u> – vv. 2-3a

"The LORD is slow to anger"

2. The LORD's <u>POWER</u> – vv. 3b-5

3. The LORD's <u>PRESENCE</u> – vv. 6-8

THE <u>REMOVAL</u> OF THE WICKED – vv. 9-15

"What do ye imagine against the LORD? He will make an utter end; affliction shall not rise up the second time. For while they are folden together like thorns, and while they are drunk like drunkards, they shall be devoured like stubble fully dry. There is one come out of thee, that imagineth evil against the LORD, a wicked counselor. Thus saith the LORD: Though they be quiet, and likewise many, yet thus shall they be cut down, when he shall pass through. Though I have afflicted thee, I will afflict thee no more. For now will I break his yoke from off thee, and will burst thy bonds in sunder. And the LORD hath given a commandment concerning thee, that no more of thy name be sown; out of the house of thy gods will I cut off the graven image and the molten image; I will make thy grave; for thou art vile. Behold upon the mountains the feet of him that bringeth good tidings, that

publisheth peace! O Judah, keep thy solemn feasts, perform thy vows; for the wicked shall no more pass through thee; he is utterly cut off."

4. The LORD's <u>PROTECTION</u> – v. 15

   (In the Hebrew text, verse 15 begins chapter 2)

THE <u>RESULTS</u> OF NINEVEH'S ATTACKS
Nahum 2:1-10

1. The <u>ATTACK</u> will come upon Nineveh – 2:1 – *"He that dasheth in pieces is come up before they face; keep the munition, watch the way, make thy loins strong, fortify thy power mightily."*

2. The <u>AVENGING</u> of the Lord will be behind it – 2:2 – *"For the LORD hath turned away the excellency of Jacob, as the excellency of Israel; for the emptiers have emptied them out, and marred their vine branches."*

3. The <u>APPEARANCE</u> of Nineveh's armies will NOT save them this time nor intimidate their attackers! vv. 3-4

"The shield of his mighty men is made red, the valiant men are in scarlet; the chariots shall be with flaming torches in the day of his preparation, and the fir trees shall be terribly shaken. The chariots shall rage in the streets, they shall justle one against another in the broad ways; they shall seem like torches, they shall run like the lightnings."

4. The <u>AUTHORITIES</u> who governed the armies for the king will panic – v. 5 – *"He shall recount his worthies; they shall stumble in their walk; they shall make haste to the wall, and the defense shall be prepared."*

5. The <u>ABILITY</u> of the wall to withstand the invasion was broken down by torrential rains and flooding – v. 6

"The gates of the rivers shall be opened, and the palace shall be dissolved."

6. The <u>ACCOMPLISHMENT</u> of Nineveh's destruction was decreed by the Lord and nothing could stop it – v. 7

"And Huzzah shall be led away captive, she shall be brought up, and her maids shall lead her as with the voice of doves, tabering upon their breasts."

7. The <u>AGONY</u> of Nineveh's losses will end their domination of the ancient world – vv. 8-10

"But Nineveh is of old like a pool of water; yet they shall flee away. Stand! Stand! Shall they cry; but none shall look back. Take the spoil of silver, take the spoil of gold; for there is none end of the store and glory out of all the pleasant furniture. She is empty, and void, and waste; and the heart melteth, and the knees smite together, and much pain is in all loins, and the faces of them all gather blackness."

THE <u>REALIZATION</u> OF WHAT GOD WILL DO!
Nahum 2:11-13

"Where is the dwelling of the lions, and the feeding place of the young lions, where the lion, even the old lion, walked, and the lion's whelp, and none made them afraid? The lion did tear in pieces enough for his whelps, and strangled for his lionesses, and filled his holes with prey, and his dens with ravin. Behold, I am against thee, saith the LORD of hosts, and I will burn her chariots in the smoke, and the sword shall devour thy young lions; and I will cut off thy prey from the earth, and the voice of thy messengers shall no more be heard."

THE <u>REVELATION</u> OF NINEVEH'S TRUE CHARACTER
Nahum 3:1-7

1. The <u>DEATH</u> of thousands was caused by the Assyrian armies – vv. 1-3

"Woe to the bloody city! It is all full of lies and robbery; the prey departeth not; The noise of a whip, and the noise of the rattling of the wheels, and of the prancing horses, and of the jumping chariots. The horseman lifteth up both the bright sword and the glittering spear; and there is a multitude of slain, and a great number of carcasses; and there is none end of their corpses; they stumble upon their corpses."

2. The **DECEPTION** of nations was caused by their involvement in the occult and sexual immorality – v. 4

"Because of the multitude of the whoredoms of the well-favored harlot, the mistress of witchcrafts, that selleth nations through her whoredoms, and families through her witchcrafts."

3. The **DECLARATION** of God against this mighty nation reveals the severity of their coming judgment – v. 5a – *"Behold, I am against thee, saith the LORD of hosts"*

4. The <u>DISPLAY</u> of Assyria's shame and filth will be seen by the world – vv. 5b-7

"I will discover thy skirts from thy face, and I will show the nations thy nakedness, and the kingdoms thy shame. And I will cast abominable filth upon thee, and make thee vile, and will set thee as a gazing-stock. And it shall come to pass that all they that look upon thee shall flee from thee, and say, Nineveh is laid waste; who will bemoan her? Whence shall I seek comforters for thee?"

THE <u>REMEMBRANCE</u> OF WHAT HAPPENED TO NO-AMON (THEBES)
Nahum 3:8-10

"Art thou better than populous No-Amon (Thebes), *that was situate among the rivers, that had the waters round about it, whose rampart was the sea, and her wall was from the sea? Ethiopia and Egypt were her strength, and it was infinite; Put and Lubim*

were thy helpers. Yet was she carried away, she went into captivity; her young children also were dashed in pieces at the top of all the streets; and they cast lots for her honorable men, and all her great men were bound in chains."

THE **REVIEW** OF NINEVEH'S DESTRUCTION –
Nahum 3:11-19

"Thou also shalt be drunk; thou shalt be hid, thou also shalt seek strength because of the enemy. All thy strongholds shall be like fig trees with the first-ripe figs; if they be shaken, they shall even fall into the mouth of the eater. Behold, thy people in the midst of thee are women; the gates of thy land shall be set wide open unto thine enemies; the fire shall devour thy bars. Draw thee waters for the siege, fortify thy strongholds; go into clay, and tread the mortar, make strong the brickkiln. There shall the fire devour thee; the sword shall cut thee off, it shall eat thee up like the cankerworm. Make thyself many like the cankerworm, make thyself many like the locusts. Thou hast multiplied thy merchants above the stars of heaven; the cankerworm spoileth, and flieth away. The crowned are like the locusts, and thy captains like the great grasshoppers, which camp in the hedges in the cold day, but when the sun ariseth they flee away, and their place is not known where they are. Thy shepherds slumber, O king of Assyria; thy nobles shall dwell in the dust; thy people are scattered upon the mountains, and no man gathereth them. There is no healing of thy bruise, thy wound is grievous; all that hear the bruit of thee shall clap the hands over thee; for upon whom hath not thy wickedness passed continually?"

WHAT WE LEARN ABOUT TO FROM THIS PROPHECY OF NAHUM!

1. God <u>CONTROLS</u> the weather and the nations of this world!

2. God <u>CAUSES</u> His judgment to fall on those who think that their power gives them the right to

commit atrocities and unjustified violence!

3. God <u>COMFORTS</u> His people by bringing His judgment on their enemies!

HABAKKUK
Habakkuk 1:1-3:19

"The burden which Habakkuk the prophet did see"

The Hebrew name means "to embrace" – the prophet was embracing difficult issues: If God is good, then why is there evil in the world? And, if there has to be evil, then why do the evil prosper? What is God doing in the world?

The date of the book is around 605 BC and Nineveh fell in 612 BC, and Babylon came to power. Egypt was in control of Judah until the Battle of Carchemish in 605 BC when Pharaoh Necho of Egypt was defeated by the Babylonians. The king of Judah was Jehoiakim (609-597 BC) – known for his wickedness.

Habakkuk was a contemporary of Jeremiah, Nahum, and Zephaniah.

THE **REACTION** OF THE PROPHET TO THE CORRUPTION OF HIS TIME!

- Habakkuk 1:2-4 – *"O LORD, how long shall I cry, and Thou wilt not hear! Even cry out unto Thee of violence, and Thou wilt not save! Why dost Thou show me iniquity, and cause me to behold grievance? For spoiling and violence are before me; and there are those who raise up strife and contention. Therefore the law is slacked, and judgment doth never go forth; for the wicked doth compass about the righteous; therefore, judgment goeth forth perverted."*

1. The <u>CRIES</u> were not being heard – v. 2

2. His <u>CONCERNS</u> were increasing – vv. 3-4

THE <u>RESPONSE</u> OF GOD TO THE PROPHET'S REACTION

Habakkuk 1:5-11 – *"Behold among the heathen, and regard, and wonder marvelously; for I will work a work in your days, which ye will not believe, though it be told you. For, lo, I raise up the Chaldeans, that bitter and hasty nation, which shall march through the breadth of the land, to possess the dwelling places that are not theirs. They are terrible and dreadful; their judgment and their dignity shall proceed from themselves. Their horses also are swifter than the leopards, and are more fierce than the evening wolves; and their horsemen shall spread themselves, and their horsemen shall come from far; they shall fly like the eagle that hasteth to eat. They shall come all for violence; their faces shall sup up as the east wind. And they shall scoff at the kings, and the princes shall be a scorn unto them; they shall deride every stronghold; for they shall heap dust, and take it. Then shall his mind change, and he shall pass over, and offend, imputing this his power unto his god."*

1. The <u>REALIZATION</u> of what God will do made it difficult for the prophet to understand – v. 5

2. The <u>RISE</u> to power by the Chaldeans was caused by the Lord – vv. 6-7

3. The <u>RECOGNITION</u> of how quickly they will attack – v. 8

4. The <u>REASON</u> for this invasion - v. 9

5. Their <u>REACTION</u> to other leaders – v. 10a

6. The <u>RESULT</u> of their attacks – v. 10b

7. The <u>REASONING</u> they will have about their successes – v. 11

THE <u>RECOGNITION</u> OF THE PROPHET AS TO THE CHARACTER AND PLAN OF GOD – Habakkuk 1:12-17

"Art Thou not from everlasting, O LORD, my God, mine Holy One? We shall not die, O LORD, Thou hast ordained them for judgment; and, O mighty God, Thou hast established

them for correction. Thou art of purer eyes than to look with favor upon, and canst not look on iniquity; Wherefore lookest Thou upon them that deal treacherously, and holdest thy tongue when the wicked devoureth the man that is more righteous than he? And makest men as the fish of the sea, as the creeping things, that have no ruler over them? They take up all of them with the angle; they catch them in their net, and gather them in their drag; therefore, they rejoice and are glad. Therefore, they sacrifice unto their net, and burn incense unto their drag, because by them their portion is fat, and their meat plenteous. Shall they, therefore, empty their net, and not spare continually to slay the nations?"

1. He <u>PROCLAIMS</u> the eternal nature of God – v. 12a

2. He <u>PROVES</u> that he believes God's promises – v. 12b

3. He <u>PONDERS</u> why God allows the wicked to prosper and escape His judging hand – vv. 13-17

THE **RELUCTANCE** OF THE PROPHET TO SPEAK UNTIL HE HEARS FROM THE LORD – Habakkuk 2:1-4

"I will stand upon my watch, and set myself upon the tower, and will watch to see what He will say unto me, and what I shall answer when I am reproved. And the LORD answered me, and said, Write the vision, and make it plain upon tables, that he may run that readeth it. For the vision is yet for an appointed time, but at the end it shall speak, and not lie; though it tarry, wait for it, because it will surely come, it will not tarry. Behold, his soul that is lifted up is not upright in him; but the just shall live by his faith."

1. The **PATIENCE** he displays reveals his character and confidence in God – v. 1

2. The **PLAINNESS** of the vision reveals that the Lord wanted all to understand His plan – vv. 2-3

3. The <u>PRINCIPLE</u> that is revealed is crucial in understanding the delays of God's plan – v. 4

THE **REASONS** WHY THE JUDGMENT OF GOD WOULD COME – Habakkuk 2:5-8

"Yea, also, because he transgresseth by wine, he is a proud man, neither keepeth at home, who enlargeth his desire as hell, and is as death, and cannot be satisfied, but gathereth unto himself all nations, and heapeth unto himself all peoples. Shall not all these take up a parable against him, and a taunting proverb against him, and say, Woe to him that increaseth that which is not his! How long? And to him that ladeth himself with thick clay! Shall they not rise up suddenly that shall bite thee, and awake that shall vex thee, and thou shalt be for booties unto them? Because thou hast spoiled many nations, all the remnant of the people shall spoil thee, because of men's blood, and for the violence of the land,

of the city, and of all that dwell therein."

1. Because of their <u>DRUNKENNESS</u> – v. 5a

2. Because of their <u>DESIRE</u> for violence that could not be satisfied – v. 5b

THE <u>REVENGE</u> THAT WOULD COME UPON THE BABYLONIANS – Habakkuk 2:6-8

1. The <u>PARABLE</u> that would be used against them – v. 6a

2. The <u>PROCLAMATION</u> that would be said about the Babylonians – v. 6b

3. The <u>PUNISHMENT</u> will come as a shock and surprise – v. 7a

4. The <u>PLUNDER</u> of the Babylonians would become the possession of others – v. 7b

THE **RESULTS** WHICH GOD WILL BRING UPON THOSE WHO SIN AGAINST HIM –
Habakkuk 2:9-20

1. <u>COVETING</u> what does not belong to you – vv. 9-11

"Woe to him that coveteth an evil covetousness to his house, that he may set his nest on high, the he may be delivered from the power of evil! Thou hast consulted shame to thy house by cutting off many peoples, and hast sinned against thy soul. For the stone shall cry out of the wall, and the beam out of the timber shall answer it."

2. <u>CONSTRUCTING</u> a city and culture with blood and iniquity – vv. 12-14

"Woe to him that buildeth a town with blood, and stablisheth city by iniquity! Behold, is it not of the LORD of hosts that the peoples shall labor in the very fire, and the people shall weary themselves for every vanity? For the earth shall be filled with the knowledge

of the glory of the LORD, as the waters cover the sea."

3. <u>COMMITTING</u> others to alcoholism and sexual immorality – vv.15-17

"Woe unto him that giveth his neighbor drink, that puttest Thy bottle to him, and makest him drunken also, that thou mayest look on their nakedness! Thou art filled with shame for glory; drink thou also, and let thy foreskin be uncovered; the cup of the LORD's right hand shall be turned unto thee, and shameful spewing shall be on thy glory. For the violence of Lebanon shall cover thee, and the spoil of beasts, which made them afraid, because of men's blood, and for the violence of the land, of the city, and of all that dwell therein."

4. <u>CONTROLLING</u> people through the lies of idolatry and pagan practices – vv. 18-20

"What profiteth the graven image that its maker hath graven it; the molten image, and a teacher of lies, that the

maker of his work trusteth in it, to make dumb idols? Woe unto him that saith to the wood, Awake; to the dumb stone, Arise, it shall teach! Behold, it is laid over with gold and silver, and there is no breath at all in the midst of it. But the LORD is in His holy temple; let all the earth keep silence before Him."

THE <u>RELIANCE</u> UPON GOD WHICH THE PROPHET DISPLAYED -
Habakkuk 3:1-16

> 1. His <u>ASSOCIATION</u> with music –
>   v. 1 – *"A prayer of Habakkuk, the prophet, upon Shigionoth"*

The only other usage of this unusual word is found in Psalm *7:1* which as the word *"Shiggaion"* in the opening description of the Psalm – it says literally *"Shiggaion of David, which he sang unto the LORD"* - this chapter in Habukkuk appears to be a prayer sung to the Lord in Israel's worship. The last verse of Habukkuk 3 (verse 19) says

"To the chief singer on my stringed instruments."

2. His <u>ATTITUDE</u> was a clear reminder of the greatness of our God – v. 2a – *"O LORD, I have heard Thy speech, and was afraid..."*

3. His <u>APPEAL</u> to the LORD was based on his confidence in Who God is and what God can do – v. 2b – *"O LORD, revive Thy work in the midst of the years, in the midst of the years make know; in wrath remember mercy."*

4. His <u>ADORATION</u> focused on the acts of God in the past – vv. 3-7

"God came from Teman, and the Holy One from Mount Paran. His glory covered the heavens, and the earth was full of His praise. And His brightness was like the light; He had horns coming out of His hand; and there was the hiding of His power. Before Him went the pestilence, and burning coals went forth at His feet. He stood, and measured the earth; He beheld, and

drove asunder the nations; and the everlasting mountains were scattered, the perpetual hills did bow; His ways are everlasting. I saw the tents of Cushan in affliction: and the curtains of the land of Midian did tremble."

5. His <u>ANALYSIS</u> of the coming judgment of God upon Judah was based on what he understood to be the anger of God – vv. 8-15

"Was the LORD displeased against the rivers? Was Thine anger against the rivers? Was Thy wrath against the sea, that Thou didst ride upon Thine horses and Thy chariots of salvation? Thy bow was made quite naked, according to the oaths of the tribes, even Thy word. Thou didst cleave the earth with rivers. The mountains saw Thee, and they trembled; the overflowing of the water passed by; the deep uttered its voice, and lifted up its hands on high. The sun and moon stood still in their habitation; at the

light of Thine arrows they went, and at the shining of thy glittering spear. Thou didst march through the land in indignation; Thou didst thresh the heathen in anger. Thou wentest forth for the salvation of Thy people, even for salvation with Thine anointed; Thou woundest the head out of the house of the wicked, by discovering the foundation unto the neck. Thou didst strike through with his own staves the head of his villages; they came out like a whirlwind to scatter me; their rejoicing was as if to devour the poor secretly. Thou didst walk through the sea with Thine horses, through the heap of great waters."

6. His <u>ABILITY</u> to fathom the power and greatness of God left him in a weakened condition – v. 16

"When I heard, my belly trembled, my lips quivered at the voice; rottenness entered into my bones, and I trembled in myself, that I might rest in the day of trouble. When He cometh up unto the people, He will invade them with His troops."

THE **REJOICING** OF THE PROPHET IN THE LORD AND HIS SALVATION –
Habakkuk 3:17-19

"Although the fig tree shall not blossom, neither shall fruit be in the vines; the labor of the olive shall fail, and the fields shall yield no meat; the flock shall be cut off from the fold, and there shall be no herd in the stalls; Yet I will rejoice in the LORD, I will joy in the God of my salvation. The LORD God is my strength, and He will make my feet like hinds' feet, and He will make me walk upon mine high places. To the chief singer on my stringed instruments."

ZEPHANIAH
Zephaniah 1:1-3:20

INTRODUCTION
Zephaniah 1:1

"The word of the LORD which came unto edaliah, the son of Amariah, the son of Hezekiah, in the days of Josiah, the son of Amon, king of Judah."

1. The <u>DEFINITION</u> of his name - *the LORD hides" or "one whom the LORD hides"*

2. His family <u>DESCENT</u> makes him a great, great grandson of King Hezekiah.

<u>NOTE:</u> In I Chronicles 3:13, Manasseh is called Hezekiah's son, but, of course, he could have had more sons.

3. The <u>DAYS</u> of his prophecy – *"in the days of Josiah the son of Amon, king of Judah."*

Josiah reigned from 641 to 609 BC. The revival occurred in 623 BC and this book had to be written before the fall of Nineveh in 614 BC.

THE **<u>CONSUMING</u>** OF EVERYTHING IN THE LAND
Zephaniah 1:2-6

"I will utterly consume all things from off the land, saith the LORD. I will consume man and beast; I will consume the fowls of the heavens, and the fish of the sea, and the stumbling blocks with the wicked; and I will cut off man from the land, saith the LORD. I will stretch out Mine hand upon Judah, and upon all the inhabitants of Jerusalem; and I will cut off the remnant of Baal from this place, and the name of the Chemarim with the priests; And those who worship the host of heaven upon the housetops; and those who worship and who swear by the LORD, and who swear by Malcam; and those who are turned back from the LORD; and those who have not sought the LORD, nor inquired for Him."

Six times the prophet makes it clear that this judgment is coming directly from the LORD Himself!

1. The <u>PROPHECY</u> was specific and extensive – vv. 2-3

2. The <u>PUNISHMENT</u> of God's people was predicted – v. 4a

3. The <u>PEOPLE</u> who would be affected are given the reasons why – vv. 4b-6

<u>NOTE:</u> The *Chemarim* were idol priests whom Josiah put down – II Kings 23:5 The Hebrew root means "black" and referred to the black garments which they wore.

The word *"Malcham"* is the same as the god *"Milcom"* of the Ammonites – also called *"Moloch"* – condemned in I Kings 11:33.

THE **CONSEQUENCES** that the Day of the LORD will bring!
Zephaniah 1:7-13

"Hold thy peace at the presence of the Lord GOD; for the day of the LORD is at hand; for the LORD hath prepared a sacrifice, He hath bid His guests. And it shall come to pass in the day of the LORD's sacrifice, that I will punish the princes, and the king's children, and all such as are clothed with strange apparel. In the same day also will I punish all those who leap on the threshold, who fill their masters' houses with violence and deceit. And it shall come to pass in that day, saith the LORD, that there shall be the noise of a cry from the fish gate, and a howling from the second quarter, and a great crashing from the hills. Howl, ye inhabitants of Maktesh; for all the merchant people are cut down, all they that bear silver are cut off. And it shall come to pass at that time, that I will search Jerusalem with candles, and punish the men that are settled on their lees, that say in their heart, The LORD will not do good, neither will He do

evil. Therefore, their goods shall become a booty, and their houses a desolation; they shall also build houses, but not inhabit them; and they shall plant vineyards, but not drink the wine of them."

1. The **PREPARATION** of a sacrifice – v. 7 – *"the LORD hath prepared a sacrifice"*

2. The **PUNISHMENT** God will bring – vv. 8-12

NOTE: The word *"Maktesh"* is not a proper name but refers to "mortar."

3. The **PLUNDERING** of the land – v. 13

THE **COMING** OF THE DAY OF THE LORD – 1:14-18

"The great day of the LORD is near, it is near. And hasteth greatly even the voice of the day of the LORD; the mighty man shall cry there bitterly. That day is a day of wrath, a day of trouble and distress, a day of wasteness and desolation, a day of

darkness and gloominess; a day of clouds and thick darkness, A day of the trumpet and alarm against the fenced cities, and against the high towers. And I will bring distress upon men, that they shall walk like blind men, because they have sinned against the LORD; and their blood shall be poured out like dust, and their flesh like the dung. Neither their silver nor their gold shall be able to deliver them in the day of the LORD's wrath, but the whole land shall be devoured by the fire of His jealousy; for He shall make even a speedy riddance of all those who dwell in the land."

The words *"the Day of the LORD"* are used 25 times (four in the NT). In Zephaniah, the words seem to speak of a future day beyond his time. The words *"in that day"* are used 115 times (43 in Isaiah) with seven usages in the New Testament. It usually refers to the coming tribulation, the coming of Messiah, and His kingdom upon earth.

Revelation 6:17 – *"The great day of His wrath is come; and who shall be able to stand?"*

1. The <u>PROPHECY</u> of it nearness – v. 14a – *"The great day of the LORD is near, it is near, and hasteth greatly"*

Isaiah 13:6 – *"Wail; for the day of the LORD is at hand; it shall come as a destruction from the Almighty."*

2. The <u>POWER</u> of God's voice will be heard – v. 14b

3. The <u>PANIC</u> that it will cause – v. 14c – *"the mighty man shall cry there bitterly"*

Isaiah 13:7-8 – *"Therefore shall all hands be faint, and every man's heart shall melt; And they shall be afraid. Pangs and sorrows shall take hold of them; they shall be in pain like a woman that travaileth. They shall be amazed one at another; their faces shall be as flames."*

Luke 21:26 – *"Men's hearts failing them for fear, and for looking after those things which are coming on the earth: for the powers of heaven shall be shaken."*

4. The <u>PICTURE</u> of the end of planet earth as we now know it – vv. 15-17

    (1) A day of <u>DECEPTION</u>

    (2) A day of <u>DISTRESS</u>

    (3) A day of <u>DESOLATION</u>

    (4) A day of <u>DARKNESS</u>

    (5) A day of <u>DESTRUCTION</u>

    (6) A day of <u>DISOBEDIENCE</u>

    (7) A day of <u>DEATH</u>

5. The <u>PLEA</u> for deliverance will not be bought – v. 18a

6. The <u>PLUNDERING</u> of the land will be caused by the LORD's jealousy – v. 18b

THE <u>CALL</u> TO REPENTANCE
Zephaniah 2:1-7

"Gather yourselves together, yea, gather together, O nation not desired, Before the decree bring forth, before the day pass like the chaff, before the fierce anger of the LORD come upon you, before the day of the LORD's anger come upon you. Seek the LORD, all ye meek of the earth, who have wrought His judgment; seek righteousness, seek meekness; it may be ye shall be hid in the day of the LORD's anger. For Gaza shall be forsaken, and Ashkelon a desolation; they shall drive out Ashdod at noonday, and Ekron shall be rooted up. Woe unto the inhabitants of the seacoast, the nation of the Cherethites! The word of the LORD is against you; O Canaan, the land of the Philistines, I will even destroy thee, that there shall be no inhabitant. And the seacoast shall be dwellings and cottages for shepherds, and folds for flocks. And the coast shall be for the remnant of the house of Judah; they shall feed thereupon; in the houses of Ashkelon

shall they lie down in the evening; for the LORD, their God. Shall visit them, and turn away their captivity."

1. The <u>PLEA</u> to gather together – 2:1-2

2. The <u>PRIORITY</u> of seeking the LORD – 2:3

3. The <u>PROPHECY</u> about the land of the Philistines – 2:4-7

THE **CONFLICTS** WITH THE PEOPLE OF GOD
Zephaniah 2:8-15

"I have heard the reproach of Moab, and the revilings of the children of Ammon, whereby they have reproached My people, and magnified themselves against their border. Therefore, as I live, saith the LORD of hosts, the God of Israel. Surely Moab shall be like Sodom, and the children of Ammon like Gomorrah, even the breeding of nettles, and salt pits, and a perpetual desolation; the residue of My people shall spoil them, and the remnant of My people shall possess

them. This shall they have for their pride, because they have reproached and magnified themselves against the people of the LORD of hosts. The LORD will be terrible unto them; for He will famish all the gods of the earth; and men shall worship Him, every one from his place, even all the isles of the heathen. Ye Ethiopians also, ye shall be slain by My sword. And He will stretch out His hand against the north, and destroy Assyria, and will make Nineveh a desolation, and dry like a wilderness. And flocks shall lie down in the midst of her, all the beasts of the nations; both the cormorant and the bittern shall lodge in the upper lintels of it; their voice shall sing in the windows; desolation shall be in the thresholds; for He shall uncover the cedar work. This is the rejoicing city that dwelt carelessly, that said in her heart, I am, and there is none beside me. How is she become a desolation, a place for beasts to lie down in! Every one that passeth by her shall hiss, and wag his hand."

1. The **ARROGANCE** of Moab and Ammon – 2:8-11

2. The **ATTACK** on Ethiopia – 2:12

3. The **APATHY** of Nineveh – 2:13-15

THE **CHALLENGE** TO GOD'S PEOPLE
Zephaniah 3:1-13

1. The **REASONS** behind this warning – vv. 1-2

"Woe to her that is filthy and polluted, to the oppressing city! She obeyed not the voice; she received not correction; she trusted not in the LORD; she drew not near to her God."

2. The **RESPONSIBILITIES** of their leaders were corrupted – vv. 3-4

"Her princes within her are roaring lions; her judges are evening wolves; they gnaw not the bones till the morrow. Her prophets are light and treacherous persons; her priests have polluted the sanctuary, they have done violence to the law."

131

3. The **RECOGNITION** of what God had done among the nations made little impact upon them – vv. 5-7

"The just LORD is in the midst of her; He will not do iniquity; every morning doth He bring His judgment to light, He faileth not; but the unjust knoweth no shame. I have cut off the nations, their towers are desolate; I made their streets waste, that none passeth by; their cities are destroyed, so that there is no man, that there is none inhabitant. I said, Surely thou wilt fear me, thou wilt receive instruction; so their dwelling should not be cut off, however I punished them; but they rose early, and corrupted all their doings."

1. He is **RIGHTEOUS** in all He does!

2. He is **HOLY** in what He does!

3. He is **FAITHFUL** to do what He has said He will do!

4. He is **LONGSUFFERING!**

4. The <u>REALIZATION</u> of God's future judgment upon the whole earth should cause them to depend upon His plan and His timing – v. 8

"Therefore, wait upon Me, saith the LORD, until the day that I rise up to the prey; for My determination is to gather the nations, that I may assemble the kingdoms, to pour upon them Mine indignation, even all My fierce anger; for all the earth shall be devoured with the fire of My jealousy."

5. The blessed <u>RESULTS</u> that God will bring in the future – vv. 9-13

"For then will I turn to the peoples a pure language, that they may all call upon the Name of the LORD, to serve Him with one consent. From beyond the rivers of Ethiopia My suppliants even the daughter of My dispersed, shall bring Mine offering. In that day shalt thou not be ashamed for all thy doings, in which thou hast transgressed against Me; for then I will take away out of the midst of thee those who rejoice in thy pride, and

thou shalt no more be haughty because of My holy mountain. I will also leave in the midst an afflicted and poor people, and they shall trust in the Name of the LORD. The remnant of Israel shall not do iniquity, nor speak lies, neither shall a deceitful tongue be found in their mouth; for they shall feed and lie down, and none shall make them afraid."

1. Their <u>WORDS</u> will be changed – v. 9

2. Their <u>WORSHIP</u> will be centered in the LORD God of Israel – v. 10

3. Their <u>WAYS</u> will be characterized by humility and not pride – v. 11

4. Their <u>WORK</u> will reflect a people who trust in the Name of the LORD – v. 12

5. Their <u>WILL</u> is conformed to the holy standards of the LORD – v. 13a

6. Their <u>WELLNESS</u> in the future will mean the provision of all their needs in an environment of real and lasting peace! v. 13b

THE **COMMITMENT** OF THE LORD TO HIS PEOPLE!
Zephaniah 3:14-20

"Sing, O daughter of Zion; shout, O Israel; be glad and rejoice with all the heart, O daughter of Jerusalem. The LORD hath taken away thy judgments, He hath cast out thine enemy; the King of Israel, even the LORD, is in the midst of thee, thou shalt not see evil any more. In that day it shall be said to Jerusalem, Fear thou not; and to Zion, Let not thine hands be slack. The LORD, thy God, in the midst of thee is mighty; He will save, He will rejoice over thee with joy; He will rest in His love, He will joy over thee with singing. I will gather those who are sorrowful for the solemn assembly, who are of thee, to whom the reproach of it was a burden. Behold, at that time I will undo all that afflict thee; and I will save her that halteth, and gather

her that was driven out; and I will get them praise and fame in every land where they have been put to shame. At that time will I bring you again, even in the time that I gather you; for I will make you a name and a praise among all peoples of the earth, when I turn back your captivity before your eyes, saith the LORD."

1. He tells them to <u>REJOICE!</u> v. 14

2. He tells them to <u>REMEMBER</u> that He has conquered their enemies! v. 15

3. He tells them to <u>RELY</u> upon His power and protection – vv. 16-17a

4. He tells them to <u>RECOGNIZE</u> what a blessing they will be to His heart – v. 17b

5. He tells them to <u>REALIZE</u> all that He will do for them in the future – vv. 18-19

6. He tells them to <u>REFLECT</u> on the time He will bring them back to their land forever! v. 20

     (1)   A time when they will <u>RETURN</u>!

     (2)   A time when they will <u>REVEAL</u> God's purpose for them!

Deuteronomy 26:19 – *"And to make thee high above all nations whom He hath made, in praise, and in name, and in honor, and that thou mayest be an holy people unto the LORD thy God, as He hath spoken."*

HAGGAI
Haggai 1:1-2:23

INTRODUCTION

Haggai 1:1 – *"In the second year of Darius, the king, in the sixth month, in the first day of the month, came the word of the LORD by Haggai, the prophet, unto Zerubbabel, the son of Shealtiel, governor of Judah, and to Joshua, the song O Jehozadak, the high priest, saying."*

1. The <u>DATE</u> when it was written – *"In the second year of Darius the king, in the sixth month, in the first day of the month* – it was **August 29, 520 BC!**

2. The <u>DELIVERY</u> of this letter – *"came the word of the LORD by Haggai the prophet"*

<u>NOTE:</u> The name *"Haggai"* means "festival" – some say it means that he was born on a given festival; however, more likely is that his name parallels the message of the book – there is a

coming "festival" or "celebration" of the coming glory and kingdom of the Messiah!

3. The <u>DESTINATION</u> of the letter – *"unto Zerubbabel the son of Shealtiel, governor of Judah, and to Joshua the son of Josedech, the high priest."*

<u>NOTE:</u> The "governors" of Judah included Sheshbazzer, son of Jehoachin, the last Jewish king in the line of David. Jehoachin's grandson, Zerubbabel, ruled from 536 to 510 BC. Zerubbabel was in the direct royal line of King David. His name means "seed of Babylon."

After Zerubbabel, Elnathan ruled the province of Judea, followed by Yeho'ezer, then Ahzai, and then Nehemiah, who ruled as governor of Judea from 445-433 BC. Judea was one of the "satrapies" of Cyrus the Great, and covered the territory known as "Babylon beyond the River" – from the Euphrates River to the Mediterranean Sea.

THE **REBUILDING** OF THE
TEMPLE – Haggai 1:2-6

"Thus speaketh the LORD of hosts, saying: This people say, The time is not come, the time that the LORD's house should be built. Then came the word of the LORD by Haggai, the prophet, saying, Is it time for you, O ye, to dwell in your ceiled houses, and this house to lie waste? Now, therefore, thus saith the LORD of hosts, Consider your ways. Ye have sown much, and bring in little; ye eat, but ye have not enough; ye drink, but ye are not filled with drink; ye clothe yourselves, but there is none warm; and he that earneth wages earneth wages to put it into a bag with holes."

1. The **IMPACT** of this message comes from the *"LORD of hosts"* (used 14 times in the book, thus emphasizing the LORD's power!)

2. The **INDIFFERENCE** of the people to the centrality of worship – v. 2b *"The time is not come, the time*

that the LORD's house should be built"

3. The <u>IMPORTANCE</u> of worship over all other pursuits – vv. 3-4

4. The <u>INSTRUCTION</u> that God's people need to hear – vv. 5-6

THE **REASON** WHY THIS PROJECT NEEDS TO BE DONE – Haggai 1:7-11

"Thus saith the LORD of hosts; Consider your ways. Go up to the mountain, and bring wood, and build the house; and I will take pleasure in it, and I will be glorified, saith the LORD. Ye looked for much and, lo, it came to little; and when ye brought it home, I did blow upon it. Why? saith the LORD of hosts, Because of Mine house that is waste, and ye run every man unto his own house. Therefore, the heaven over you is stayed from dew, and the earth is stayed from her fruit. And I called for a drought upon the land, and upon the mountains, and upon the corn, and upon the new wine, and upon the oil, and upon that which the ground bringeth forth, and upon men, and

upon cattle, and upon all the labor of the hands."

THE <u>RESPONSE</u> OF THE PEOPLE
Haggai 1:12-15

"Then Zerubbabel, the son of Shealtiel, and Joshua, the son of Jehozadak, the high priest, with all the remnant of the people, obeyed the voice of the LORD, their God, and the words of Haggai, the prophet, as the LORD, their God, had sent him, and the people did fear before the LORD. Then spoke Haggai, the LORD's messenger, in the LORD's message unto the people, saying, I am with you, saith the LORD. And the LORD stirred up the spirit of Zerubbabel, the son of Shealtiel, governor of Judah, and the spirit of Joshua, the son of Jehozadak, the high priest, and the spirit of all the remnant of the people; and they came and did work in the house of the LORD of hosts, their God. In the four and twentieth day of the sixth month, in the second year of Darius, the king."

1. The **PEOPLE** obeyed the voice of the LORD their God – v. 12a

2. The **PROPHET** was accepted as a true messenger from the LORD – v. 12b

3. The **PRIORITY** of the LORD Himself was clearly understood – v. 12c

4. The **PRESENCE** of the LORD was with them again – v. 13

5. The **POWER** of the LORD was evident in the response of the leaders and all the people – v. 14

6. The **PROJECT** began only 23 days after Haggai's message – v. 15

THE **REVELATION** OF FUTURE GLORY – Haggai 2:1-9

"In the seventh month, in the one and twentieth day of the month, came the word of the LORD by the prophet Haggai, saying, Speak now to Zerubbabel, the son of Shealtiel, governor of Judah, and to Joshua, the

son of Jehozadak, the high priest, and to the residue of the people, saying, Who is left among you that saw this hour in its first glory? And how do ye see it now? Is it not in your eyes in comparison with it as nothing? Yet now be strong, O Zerubbabel, saith the LORD; and be strong, O Joshua, son of Jehozadak, the high priest; and be strong, all ye people of the land, saith the LORD, and work; for I am with you, saith the LORD of hosts. According to the word that I have covenanted with you when ye came out of Egypt, so My Spirit remaineth among you; fear not. For thus saith the LORD of hosts: Yet once, it is a little while, and I will shake the heavens, and the earth, and the sea, and the dry land; And I will shake all nations, and the Desire of all nations shall come; and I will fill this house with glory, saith the LORD of hosts. The silver is Mine, and the gold is Mine, saith the LORD of hosts. The glory of this latter house shall be greater than of the former, saith the LORD of hosts; and in this place will I give peace, saith the LORD of hosts."

1. The <u>COMMUNICATION</u> of this message was directed to the leaders and the people – v. 2

2. The <u>COMPARISON</u> with the Temple of Solomon that was destroyed – v. 3

3. The <u>CHALLENGE</u> to work – v. 4

4. The <u>COVENANT</u> of God was still in force – v. 5

5. The <u>CATASTROPHE</u> which is coming – vv. 6-7a

6. The <u>COMING</u> of the Desire of all nations and its spectacular result – v. 7b

7. The <u>CONSTRUCTION</u> of the latter house will be glorious – vv. 8-9a

8. The <u>CONTENTMENT</u> will come from the LORD of hosts – v. 9b

THE <u>REMINDER</u> OF GOD'S BLESSING – Haggai 2:10-19

1. The **PROBLEM** of uncleanness that was affecting the place of worship – vv. 11-14

"Thus saith the LORD of hosts: Ask now the priests concerning the law, saying, If one bear holy flesh in the skirt of his garment, and with his skirt do touch bread, or pottage, or wine, or oil, or any meat, shall it be holy; And the priests answered and said, No. Then said Haggai, If one that is unclean by a dead body touch any of these, shall it be unclean? And the priests answered and said, It shall be unclean. Then answered Haggai, and said, So is this people, and so is this nation before Me, saith the LORD; and so is every work of these hands, and that which they offer there is unclean."

2. The **PRODUCTIVITY** of their labors revealed the problem of their uncleanness – vv. 15-17a

"And now, I pray you, consider from this day and upward, from before a stone was laid upon a stone in the temple of the LORD; Since those days were, when one came to an heap of

twenty measures, there were but ten; when one came to the pressfat to draw out fifty vessels out of the press, there were but twenty. I smote you with blasting and with mildew and with hail in all the labors of our hands"

3. The **PREREQUISITE** for all worship was missing – v. 17b

"yet ye turned not to Me, saith the LORD"

4. The **PLEA** to consider carefully what has happened since the foundation of the temple was laid – vv. 18-19a

"Consider now from this day and upward, from the four and twentieth day of the sixth month, even from the day that the foundation of the LORD's temple was laid, consider it. Is the seed yet in the barn? Yea, as yet the vine, and the fig tree, and the pomegranate, and the olive tree"

5. The **PROCLAIMING** of future blessing from the LORD – v. 19b *"from this day will I bless you"*

THE **RESTATING** OF GOD'S PROPHETIC PLAN – Haggai 2:20-23

"And again the word of the LORD came unto Haggai in the four and twentieth day of the month, saying, Speak to Zerubbabel, governor of Judah, saying, I will shake the heavens and the earth; And I will overthrow the throne of kingdoms, and I will destroy the strength of the kingdoms of the heathen; and I will overthrow the chariots, and those who ride in them; and the horses and their riders shall come down, every one by the sword of his brother. In that day, saith the LORD of hosts, will I take thee, O Zerubbabel, My servant, the son of Shealtiel, saith the LORD, and will make thee as a signet; for I have chosen thee, saith the LORD of hosts."

1. It involves the **SHAKING** of the heavens and the earth – v. 21

2. It involves the **SMASHING** of the Gentile kingdoms – v. 22

3. It involves the **SERVANT** of the LORD – v. 23

ZECHARIAH

Zechariah 1:1-14:21

INTRODUCTION

Zechariah 1:1 – *"In the eighth month, in the second year of Darius, came the word of the LORD unto Zechariah, the son of Berechiah, the son of Iddo, the prophet, saying"*

The <u>PERIOD</u> of time – *"in the eight month, in the second year of Darius"*

The time would be 520 BC, contemporary with the message of Haggai.

Persian texts record a western campaign by Darius in the winter of 519-518 BC, which included the Land of Israel. He went on to Egypt where he put down a rebellion by the end of November in 518 BC.

The <u>PROPHET</u> involved – *"came the word of the LORD unto Zechariah, the son of Berechiah, the son of Iddo the prophet"*

His name means "the LORD remembers" – His father's name (Berechiah) means "The LORD blesses" and apparently he had died young leaving Zechariah's grandfather, Iddo, to raise him. According to Nehemiah 12:4, Iddo was a priest.

<u>INVITATION</u> to repentance
Zechariah 1:2-6

"The LORD hath been sore displeased with your fathers. Therefore, say thou unto them, Thus saith the LORD of hosts, Turn unto Me, saith the LORD of hosts, and I will turn unto you, saith the LORD of hosts. Be not as your fathers, unto whom the former prophets have cried, saying, Thus saith the LORD of hosts: Turn now from your evil ways, and from your evil doings; but they did not hear, nor hearken unto Me, saith the LORD. Your fathers, where are they? And the prophets, do they live forever? But My words and My statutes, which I commanded My servants, the prophets, did they not take hold of your fathers? And they returned and

said, As the LORD of hosts thought to do unto us, according to our ways and according to our doings, so hath He dealt with us."

1. The <u>PROBLEM</u> stated – v. 2 – *"The LORD hath been sore displeased with your fathers"*

2. The <u>PLEA</u> given – v. 3 – *"Turn ye unto Me, saith the LORD of hosts, and I will turn unto you, saith the LORD of hosts."*

<u>NOTE:</u> The term *"LORD of hosts"* appears three times in this one verse! It is used 261 times in the Old Testament, 38 of which are in Haggai, 53 in Zechariah, and 24 in Malachi.

Deuteronomy 4:30-31 – *"...if thou turn to the LORD thy God, and shalt be obedient unto His voice...He will not forsake thee, neither destroy thee, nor forget the covenant of thy fathers which He sware unto them."*

II Chronicles 15:4 – *"But when they in their trouble did turn unto the*

LORD God of Israel, and sought Him, He was found of them."

Isaiah 44:22 – "I have blotted out, as a thick cloud, thy transgressions, and, as a cloud, thy sins: return unto Me, for I have redeemed thee."

Isaiah 55:7 – "Let the wicked forsake his way, and the unrighteous man his thoughts; and let him return unto the LORD, and He will have mercy upon him; and to our God, for He will abundantly pardon."

Ezekiel 18:30 – "Repent, and turn yourselves from all your transgressions; so iniquity shall not be your ruin."

Hosea 6:1 – "Come, and let us return unto the LORD: for He hath torn, and He will heal us."

Hosea 14:1 – "O Israel, return unto the LORD thy God; for thou hast fallen by thine iniquity."

Joel 2:12-13 – "Turn ye even to Me with all your heart, and with *fasting, and with weeping, and with mourning: And rend your heart, and not your garments, and turn unto the LORD your God: for He is gracious and merciful, slow to anger, and of great kindness, and repenteth Him of the evil."*

Malachi 3:7 – *"Return unto Me, and I will return unto you, saith the LORD of hosts."*

3. The <u>PAST</u> remembered – vv. 4-5

> **(1) Their <u>FATHERS</u> were not an example to follow!**

> **(2) The <u>FAILURE</u> to hear and obey was the heart of their problem!**

> **(3) The <u>FATE</u> of their fathers will one day be theirs!**

> **(4) The <u>FAITHFULNESS</u> of the prophets will not always be there!**

4. The <u>PLAN</u> for repentance – v. 6

(1) It was based on the <u>WORD</u> of God!

(2) It was based on the <u>WILL</u> of God!

(3) It was based on the <u>WORK</u> of God in dealing with them!

<u>ILLUMINATION</u> through visions
Zechariah 1:7-6:15

God's <u>PLAN</u> for Jerusalem – vv. 7-21

VISION OF <u>COMFORT</u> – 1:7-17

1. The <u>PICTURE</u> of a man upon a red horse – 1:8 – *"He stood among the myrtle trees"*

<u>NOTE:</u> The *"myrtle trees"* are fragrant shrubs that reach the size of trees – used in the celebration of the Feast of Sukkot (Tabernacles) and in betrothal celebrations (according to the Encyclopedia Judaica). They are always green and give off a very

fragrant smell – most commentators say they are symbols of the Nation of Israel.

    2. The <u>PERPLEXITY</u> of the prophet – v. 8a – *"O my lord, what are these?"*

    3. The <u>PROBLEM</u> of the red horses behind the man – vv. 8b, 10-11

<u>NOTE:</u> The Hebrew word *"speckled"* is used only here and appears to be a mixture, like "reddish brown."

    4. The <u>PROTECTION</u> of God's people – vv. 12-14

"Then the angel of the LORD answered and said, O LORD of hosts, how long wilt thou not have mercy on Jerusalem and on the cities of Judah, against which thou hast had indignation these threescore and ten years? And the LORD answered the angel that talked with me with good words and comfortable words. So the angel that communed with me said unto me, Cry thou, saying, Thus saith the LORD of

hosts: I am jealous for Jerusalem and for Zion with a great jealousy."

 5. The <u>PUNISHMENT</u> of the nations – v. 15

"And I am very sore displeased with the heathen that are at ease; for I was but a little displeased, and they helped forward the affliction."

 6. The <u>PROMISES</u> to God's people – vv. 16-17

"Therefore, thus saith the LORD; I am returned to Jerusalem, with mercies; My house shall be built in it, saith the LORD of hosts, and a line shall be stretched forth upon Jerusalem. Cry yet, saying, Thus saith the LORD of hosts: My cities through prosperity shall yet be spread abroad, and the LORD shall yet comfort Zion, and shall yet choose Jerusalem."

VISION OF <u>CONQUEST</u> – 1:18-21

"Then lifted I up mine eyes, and saw, and behold four horns. And I said unto the angel who talked with me, What *are these? And he answered me, These are the horns which have scattered Judah, Israel, and Jerusalem. And the LORD showed me four carpenters. Then said I, What come these to do? And he spoke, saying, These are the horns which have scattered Judah, so that no man did lift up his head; but these are come to fray them, to cast out the horns of the Gentiles, which lifted up their horn over the land of Judah to scatter it."*

1. The <u>DISPERSION</u> of God's people – vv. 18-19

2. The <u>DESTRUCTION</u> of those nations (carpenters) – vv. 20-21

God's <u>PROTECTION</u> of His people

Zechariah 2:1-13

1. The <u>DECISION</u> to measure Jerusalem – Zechariah 2:1-3

"I lifted up mine eyes again, and looked, and behold a man with a measuring line in his hand. Then said

*I, Whither goest thou? And he said
unto me, To measure Jerusalem, to see
what is the breadth of it, and is its
length. And, behold, the angel who
talked with me went forth, and another
angel went out to meet him."*

2. The <u>DECREE</u> from the angel –
   vv. 4-5

*"And said unto him, Run, speak to this
young man, saying, Jerusalem shall be
inhabited like towns without walls for
the multitude of men and cattle in it;
For I, saith the LORD, will be unto it a
wall of fire round about, and will be
the glory in the midst of it."*

3. The <u>DELIVERANCE</u> of God's
   people – vv. 6-7

*"Ho, ho, come forth, and flee from the
land of the north, saith the LORD; for I
have spread you abroad as the four
winds of the heavens, saith the LORD.
Deliver thyself, O Zion, that dwellest
with the daughter of Babylon."*

4. The <u>DESTRUCTION</u> of the nations
   – vv. 8-9

"For thus saith the LORD of hosts: After the glory hath He sent me unto the nations which spoiled you; for He that toucheth you toucheth the apple of His eye. For, behold, I will shake Mine hand upon them, and they shall be a spoil to their servants; and ye shall know that the LORD of hosts hath sent me."

5. The <u>DELIGHT</u> of God's people – vv. 10-13

    (1)   As to God's <u>PROMISE</u> – v. 10

"Sing and rejoice, O daughter of Zion; for, lo, I come, and I will dwell in the midst of thee, saith the LORD."

    (2)   As to God's <u>PLAN</u> for the nations – v. 11a

"And many nations shall be joined to the LORD in that day…"

    (3)   As to God's <u>PEOPLE</u> – v. 11b

"and shall be My people"

(4) As to God's <u>PRESENCE</u> –
v. 11c

"and I will dwell in the midst of thee"

(5) As to God's <u>PROOF</u> –
v. 11d

"and thou shalt know that the LORD of hosts hath sent Me unto thee"

(6) As to God's <u>PORTION</u> –
v. 12

"And the Lord shall inherit Judah as His portion in the holy land, and shall choose Jerusalem again."

(7) As to God's <u>POWER</u> –
v. 13

"Be silent, O all flesh, before the LORD; for He is raised up out of His holy habitation."

GOD'S <u>PRESENCE</u> AMONG HIS PEOPLE!
Zechariah 3:1-10

1. The **PREPARATION** for His coming – vv. 1-7

"And he showed me Joshua, the high priest, standing before the angel of the LORD, and Satan standing at his right hand to resist him. And the LORD said unto Satan, The LORD rebuke thee, O Satan; even the LORD, Who hath chosen Jerusalem, rebuke thee. Is not this a brand plucked out of the fire? Now Joshua was clothed with filthy garments, and stood before the angel. And he answered and spoke unto those who stood before him, saying, Take away the filthy garments from him. And unto him He said, Behold, I have caused thine iniquity to pass from thee, and I will clothe thee with change of raiment. And I said, Let them set a clean turban upon his head. So they set a fair mitre upon his head, and clothed him with garments. And the angel of the LORD stood by. And the angel of the LORD protested unto Joshua, saying, Thus saith the LORD of hosts, If thou wilt walk in My ways, and if thou wilt keep My charge, then thou shalt also judge My house, and

shalt also keep My courts, and I will give thee places to walk among these who stand by."

  (1) The <u>CONFLICT</u> facing them – v. 1

  (2) The <u>CHOICE</u> of God – v. 2

  (3) The <u>CONDITION</u> of Joshua – v. 3 – *"clothed with filthy garments"*

  (4) The <u>CLEANSING</u> of Joshua – v. 4a

  (5) The <u>CLOTHING</u> he needed – vv. 4b-5

  (6) The <u>COMMANDS</u> to be kept – vv. 6-7

2. The <u>PURPOSE</u> of His coming – vv. 8-10

"Hear now, O Joshua, the high priest, thou, and thy fellows who sit before thee; for they are men wondered at; for, behold, I will bring forth My servant, the BRANCH. For, behold, the

stone that I have laid before Joshua; upon one stone shall be seven eyes; behold, I will engrave the graving of it, saith the LORD of hosts, and I will remove the iniquity of that land in one day. In that day, saith the LORD of hosts, shall ye call every man his neighbor under the vine and under the fig tree."

1. He is the <u>SERVANT</u>!

2. He is the <u>STONE</u>!

3. He is the <u>SAVIOR</u>!

4. He is the <u>SUPPLY</u> for all our needs!

GOD'S <u>POWER</u> FOR HIS PEOPLE!
Zechariah 4:1-14

1. The <u>PURPOSE</u> for involvement in the work of the LORD – 4:1-6a

"And the angel who talked with me came again, and waked me, as a man that is wakened out of his sleep, and said unto me, What seest thou? And I

said, I have looked and, behold, a candlestick all of gold, with a bowl upon the top of it, and its seven lamps on it, and seven pipes to the seven lamps, which are upon the top of it, and two olive trees by it, one upon the right side of the bowl, and the other upon the left side of it. So I answered and spoke to the angel who talked with me, saying, What are these, my lord? Then the angel who talked with me answered and spake unto me, Knowest thou not what these are? And I said, No, my lord. Then he answered and spoke unto me, saying, This is the word of the LORD unto Zerubbabel..."

2. The **POWER** by which the work of God is accomplished – vv. 6b-10

     (1)   No **DEPENDENCE** upon human strength – v. 6b

"Not by might, nor by power, but by My Spirit, saith the LORD of hosts"

     (2)   No **DIFFICULTIES** too great to overcome – v. 7

"Who art thou, O great mountain? Before Zerubbabel thou shalt become a plain; and he shall bring forth the headstone of it with shoutings, crying, Grace, grace unto it."

> (3) No **DISAPPOINTMENT** as to what God can do! vv. 8-10

"Moreover, the word of the LORD came unto me, saying, The hands of Zerubbabel have laid the foundation of this house; his hands shall also finish it, and thou shalt know that the LORD of hosts hath sent me unto you. For who hath despised the day of small things? For they shall rejoice, and shall see the plummet in the hand of Zerubbabel with those seven; they are the eyes of the LORD; which run to and fro through the whole earth."

> 3. The **PERSON** for Whom the work is done! – vv. 11-14

"Then answered I, and said unto him, What are these two olive trees; upon the right side of the candlestick and upon the left side of it? And I answered

again, and said unto him, What are these two olive branches which, through the two golden pipes, empty the golden oil out of themselves? And he answered me and said, Knowest thou not what these are? And I said, No, my lord. Then said he, These are the two anointed ones, that stand by the Lord of the whole earth."

GOD'S **PREDICTIONS** ABOUT THE FUTURE – Zechariah 5:1-11

1. **DISOBEDIENCE** to God's moral standards – vv. 1-4

"Then I turned, and lifted up mine eyes, and looked, and behold a flying roll. And he said unto me, What seest thou? And I answered, I see a flying roll, its length is twenty cubits, and its breadth ten cubits. Then said he unto me, This is the curse that goeth forth over the face of the whole earth; for every one that stealeth shall be cut off as on this side according to it; and every one that sweareth shall be cut off as on that side according to it. I will bring it forth, saith the LORD of hosts, and it shall

enter into the house of the thief, and into the house of him that sweareth falsely by My name; and it shall remain in the midst of his house, and shall consume it with its timber and its stones."

2. <u>DECAY</u> of religion – vv. 5-8

"Then the angel who talked with me went forth, and said unto me, Lift up now thine eyes, and see what is this that goeth forth. And I said, What is it? And he said, This is an ephah that goeth forth. He said, moreover, This is their resemblance through all the earth. And, behold, there was lifted up a talent of lead; and this is a woman that sitteth in the midst of the ephah. And he said, This is wickedness. And he cast it into the midst of the ephah; and he cast the weight of lead upon the mouth of it."

3. <u>DEVELOPMENT</u> of the final world empire – vv. 9-11

"Then lifted I up mine eyes, and looked and, behold, there came out two women, and the wind was in their

wings; for they had wings like the wings of a stork, and they lifted up the ephah between the earth and the heaven. Then said I to the angel who talked with me, Whither do these bear the ephah? And he said unto me, To build for it an house in the land of Shinar; and it shall be established, and set there upon its own base."

GOD'S **PROMISE** TO HIS PEOPLE
Zechariah 6:1-15

1. The <u>DESTINY</u> of the nations –
   6:1-8

   (1) The <u>SYMBOL</u> of the chariots – v. 1a – *"there came four chariots"*

   (2) The <u>SCENE</u> involving two mountains – v. 1b

   (3) The <u>SIGNIFICANCE</u> of the colors – vv. 2-3

"Before the first chariot were red horses; and before the second chariot, black horses; And before the third

chariot, white horses; and before the fourth chariot grisled and bay horses."

  (4)   The <u>**SPIRITS**</u> of the heavens – vv. 4-5

"Then I answered and said unto the angel who talked with me, What are these, my lord? And the angel answered and said unto me, These are the four spirits of the heavens, which go forth from standing before the Lord of all the earth."

  (5)   The <u>**SITES**</u> where they go – v. 6

"The black horses which are there go forth into the north country; and the white go forth after them; and the grisled go forth toward the south country."

  (6)   The <u>**SOVEREIGNTY**</u> that they manifest – v. 7

"And the bay went forth, and sought to go that they might walk to and fro through the earth; and he said, Get you hence, walk to and fro through the

earth. So they walked to and fro through the earth."

          (7)   The <u>SILENCE</u> of the north country – v. 8

"Then cried he to me, and spoke unto me, saying, Behold, these that go toward the north country have quieted my spirit in the north country."

    2. The <u>DOMINION</u> of the Messiah – 6:9-15

          (1)   The <u>CROWNING</u> of Joshua, the High Priest – vv. 9-11

"And the word of the LORD came unto me, saying, Take of them of the captivity, even of Heldai, of Tobijah, and of Jedaiah, who are come from Babylon, and come the same day, and go into the house of Josiah, the son of Zephaniah. Then take silver and gold, and make crowns, and set them upon the head of Joshua, the son of Jehoiadak, the High Priest."

(2) The <u>COMING</u> of the BRANCH – v. 12

"And speak unto him, saying, Thus speaketh the LORD of hosts; saying, Behold, the man whose name is the BRANCH; and He shall grow up out of His place, and He shall build the temple of the LORD;"

(3) The <u>CHARACTER</u> of the Branch – v. 13

"Even He shall build the temple of the LORD; and He shall bear the glory, and shall sit and rule upon His throne; and He shall be a priest upon His throne; and the counsel of peace shall be between them both."

(4) The <u>CONSTRUCTION</u> of the temple – vv. 14-15

"And the crowns shall be to Helem, and to Tobijah, and to Jedaiah, and to Hen, the son of Zephaniah, for a memorial in the temple of the LORD. And they that are far off shall come and build in the temple of the LORD, and ye shall know that the LORD of hosts hath sent

Me unto you. And this shall come to pass, if ye will diligently obey the voice of the LORD, your God."

<u>INSTRUCTION</u> concerning fasts – Zechariah 7:1-8:23

The only fast required by the Law of Moses was *Yom Kippur*, the Day of Atonement – Leviticus 23:26-32

During the captivity to Babylon, the Jewish people practiced four fasts:

> The *"fourth month"* – the capture of Jerusalem by Babylon
>
> The *"fifth month"* – the burning of the city and the temple
>
> The *"seventh month"* – the murder of Gedaliah
>
> The *"tenth month"* – the siege against Jerusalem by Nebuchadnezzar

1. The <u>INQUIRY</u> from Babylon – 7:1-3

"And it came to pass in the fourth year of King Darius, that the word of the LORD came unto Zechariah in the fourth day of the ninth month, even in Chislev, When they had sent unto the house of God Sharezer and Regemmelech, and their men, to pray before the LORD, and to speak unto the priests who were in the house of the LORD of hosts, and to the prophets, saying, Should I weep in the fifth month, separating myself, as I have done these so many years?"

2. The <u>INTENTION</u> behind it – 7:4-7

"Then came the word of the LORD of hosts unto me, saying, Speak unto all the people of the land, and to the priests, saying, When ye fasted and mourned in the fifth and seventh month, even those seventy years, did ye at all fast unto Me, even to Me? And when ye did eat, and what ye did drink, did not ye eat for yourselves, and drink for yourselves? Should ye not hear the words which the LORD hath cried by the former prophets, when Jerusalem was inhabited and in

*prosperity, and its cities round about
it, when men inhabited the south and
the plain?*

     (1)   As to the <u>NATURE</u> of
           their religious
           observances – *"did ye at
           all fast unto Me...?"*

     (2)   As to the <u>NECESSITIES</u>
           of life – *"when ye did eat
           and when ye did drink"*
           – was this for
           yourselves?

     (3)   As to the <u>NEED</u> of
           remembering the word
           of the LORD – v. 7

3. The <u>INSTRUCTION</u> that is needed
  – vv. 8-10

*"And the word of the LORD came unto
Zechariah, saying, Thus speaketh the
LORD of hosts, saying, Execute true
judgment, and show mercy and
compassions, every man to his
brother; And oppress not the widow,
nor the fatherless, the stranger, nor*

the poor; and let none of you imagine evil against his brother in your heart."

4. The __INDIFFERENCE__ of their response – vv. 11-14

"But they refused to hearken, and pulled away the shoulder, and stopped their ears, that they should not hear. Yea, they made their hearts as an adamant stone, lest they should hear the law, and the words which the LORD of hosts hath sent in His Spirit by the former prophets; therefore came a great wrath from the LORD of hosts. Therefore, it is come to pass that, as He cried, and they would not hear, so they cried, and I would not hear, saith the LORD of hosts; But I scattered them with a whirlwind among all the nations whom they knew not. Thus the land was desolate after them, that no man passed through nor returned; for they laid the pleasant land desolate."

(1)   They __REFUSED__ to listen!

(2)   They __RESISTED__ what God had to say!

(3)   The <u>REASON</u> for the
wrath of the LORD!

(4)   The <u>RESULTS</u> which the
LORD of hosts brought!

5. The <u>IMPACT</u> of God's care and
concern – 8:1-23

(1)   The <u>COMPASSION</u> He
revealed – vv. 1-3

*"Again the word of the LORD of hosts
came to me, saying, Thus saith the
LORD of hosts: I was jealous for Zion
with great jealousy, and I was jealous
for her with great fury. Thus saith the
LORD: I am returned unto Zion, and
will dwell in the midst of Jerusalem;
and Jerusalem shall be called a city of
truth, and the mountain of the LORD of
hosts; the holy mountain."*

(2)   The <u>CHARACTER</u> of
those days – vv. 4-6

*"Thus saith the LORD of hosts: There
shall yet old men and old women dwell
in the streets of Jerusalem, and every
man with his staff in his hand for very*

age. And the streets of the city shall be full of boys and girls playing in the streets of it. Thus saith the LORD of hosts: If it be marvelous in the eyes of the remnant of this people in these days, should it also be marvelous in Mine eyes? saith the LORD of hosts."

> (3) God's <u>COMMITMENT</u> to His people – vv. 7-8

"Thus saith the LORD of hosts; Behold, I will save My people from the east country, and from the west country; And I will bring them, and they shall dwell in the midst of Jerusalem; and they shall be My people, and I will be their God, in truth and in righteousness."

> (4) The <u>CHALLENGE</u> for His people – vv. 9-17

"Thus saith the LORD of hosts; Let your hands be strong, ye that hear in these days these words by the mouth of the prophets, who were in the day that the foundation of the house of the LORD of hosts was laid, that the temple might be built. For before these days

there was no hire for man, nor any hire for beast, neither was there any peace to him that went out or came in because of the affliction; for I set all men, every one, against his neighbor. But now I will not be unto the residue of this people as in the former days, saith the LORD of hosts. For the seed shall be prosperous; the vine shall give its fruit, and the ground shall give its increase, and the heavens shall give their dew; and I will cause the remnant of this people to possess all these things. And it shall come to pass that, as ye were a curse among the heathen, O house of Judah and house of Israel, so will I save you, and ye shall be a blessing; fear not, but let your hands be strong. For thus saith the LORD of hosts; As I thought to punish you, when your fathers provoked Me to wrath, saith the LORD of hosts, and I repented not, So again have I thought in these days to do well unto Jerusalem, and to the house of Judah; fear ye not. These are the things that ye shall do: Speak every man the truth to his neighbor; execute the judgment of truth and peace in your gates; And *let none of you imagine evil in your hearts against his neighbor; and love no false oath; for all these are things that I hate, saith the LORD."*

(5) The <u>COMING</u> of many people to the LORD — vv. 18-23

"And the word of the LORD of hosts came unto me, saying, Thus saith the LORD of hosts; The fast of the fourth month, and the fast of the fifth, and the fast of the seventh, and the fast of the tenth, shall be to the house of Judah joy and gladness, and cheerful feasts; therefore, love the truth and peace. Thus saith the LORD of hosts: It shall yet come to pass that there shall come peoples, and the inhabitants of many cities; And the inhabitants of one city shall go to another, saying, Let us go speedily to pray before the LORD, and to seek the LORD of hosts; I will go also. Yea, many peoples and strong nations shall come to seek the LORD of hosts in Jerusalem, and to pray before the LORD. Thus saith the LORD of hosts: In those days it shall come to

pass that ten men shall take hold out of all languages of the nations, even shall take hold of the skirt of him that is a Jew, saying, We will go with you; for we have heard that God is with you."

<u>INVITATION</u> to repentance – Zechariah 1:1-6

<u>ILLUMINATION</u> through visions - Zechariah 1:7-6:15

<u>INSTRUCTION</u> concerning fasts - Zechariah 7:1-8:23

<u>INTRODUCTION</u> to future events!
Zechariah 9:1-14:21

The <u>DEFENSE</u> of Israel – 9:1-10:12

    1. <u>VENGEANCE</u> on her enemies – 9:1-8

        (1) <u>SYRIAN</u> territories – vv. 1-4

"The burden of the word of the LORD in the land of Hadrach, and Damascus shall be its rest, when the eyes of man,

as of all the tribes of Israel, shall be toward the LORD. And Hamath, also shall border by it; Tyre, and Sidon, though it be very wise. And Tyre did build herself a stronghold, and heaped up silver like the dust, and fine gold like the mire of the streets. Behold, the Lord will cast her out, and He will smite her power in the sea, and she shall be devoured with fire."

HADRACH
HAMATH

(2)   PHILISTINE territories
        – vv. 5-8

"Ashkelon shall see it, and fear; Gaza also shall see it, and be very sorrowful, and Ekron; for her expectation shall be ashamed; and the king shall perish from Gaza, and Ashkelon shall not be inhabited. And a bastard shall dwell in Ashdod, and I will cut off the pride of the Philistines. And I will take away his blood out of his mouth, and his abominations from between his teeth; but he that remaineth, even he, shall be for our God, and he shall be like a governor in Judah, and Ekron like a

Jebusite. And I will encamp about Mine house because of the army, because of him that passeth by, and because of him that returneth; and no oppressor shall pass through them any more; for now have I seen with mine eyes."

EKRON
GAZA
ASHKELON
ASHDOD

2. <u>VICTORY</u> through the LORD!
   9:9-17

    (1) <u>REJOICING</u> over His coming – v. 9

"Rejoice greatly, O daughter of Zion; shout, O daughter of Jerusalem; behold, thy King cometh unto thee; He is just, and having salvation; lowly, and riding upon an ass and upon a colt, the foal of an ass."

    (2) <u>REVENGE</u> through His people – vv. 10-15

"And I will cut off the chariot from Ephraim, and the horse from Jerusalem, and the battle bow shall be cut off; and He shall speak peace unto the heathen; and His dominion shall be from sea even to sea, and from the river even to the ends of the earth. As for thee also, by the blood of thy covenant I have sent forth thy prisoners out of the pit in which is no water. Turn to the stronghold, ye prisoners of hope; even today do I declare that I will render double unto thee. When I have bent Judah for Me, filled the bow with Ephraim, and raised up thy sons, O Zion, against thy sons, O Greece, and made thee like the sword of a mighty man. And the LORD shall be seen over them, and His arrow shall go forth like the lightning; and the Lord GOD shall blow the trumpet, and shall go with whirlwinds of the south. The LORD of hosts shall defend them; and they shall devour, and subdue with sling-stones; and they shall drink, and make a noise as through wine; and they shall be filled like bowls, and like the corners of the altar.

(3)   RESTORATION of His people – v. 16

And the LORD, their God, shall save them in that day as the flock of His people; for they shall be like the stones of a crown, lifted up as an ensign upon His land."

(4)   RESPONSE to His greatness – v. 17

For how great is His goodness, and how great is His beauty! Corn shall make the young men cheerful, and new wine, the maids."

3. VANITY of idols and shepherds – 10:1-3

"Ask of the LORD rain in the time of the latter rain; so the LORD shall make bright clouds, and give them showers of rain, to every one grass in the field. For the idols have spoken vanity, and the diviners have seen a lie, and have told false dreams; they comfort in vain; therefore, they went their way like a flock; they were troubled, because there was no shepherd. Mine

*anger was kindled against the
shepherds, and I punished the goats;
for the LORD of hosts hath visited His
flock, the house of Judah, and hath
made them as His goodly horse in the
battle."*

4. <u>VISION</u> of their return – 10:4-12

(1) It is the <u>PERSON</u> of the
Messiah Who will
accomplish it! vv. 4-5

*"Out of Him came forth the corner, out
of Him the nail, out of Him the battle
bow, out of Him every oppressor
together. And they shall be like mighty
men, who tread down their enemies in
the mire of the streets in the battle; and
they shall fight."*

(2) It is the <u>PRESENCE</u> of
the LORD that will make
them mighty in battle –
v. 5b

*"because the LORD is with them, and
the riders on horses shall be
confounded."*

(3) It is the <u>POWER</u> of God that will enable His people to gain the victory and return – v. 6a

"And I will strengthen the house of Judah, and I will save the house of Joseph, and I will bring them again to place them;"

(4) It is the <u>PROMISE</u> of God that cannot be broken – v. 6b

"for I have mercy upon them, and they shall be as though I had not cast them off; for I am the LORD, their God, and will hear them."

(5) It is the <u>PRAISE</u> of His people that He desires – v. 7

"And they of Ephraim shall be like a mighty man, and their heart shall rejoice as through wine; yea, their children shall see it, and be glad; their heart shall rejoice in the LORD."

(6) It is the <u>PLAN</u> of God that will bring it to pass – vv. 8-12

"I will hiss for them, and gather them; for I have redeemed them, and they shall increase as they have increased. And I will sow them among the peoples; and they shall remember Me in far countries, and they shall live with their children, and turn again. I will bring them again also out of the land of Egypt, and gather them out of Assyria; and I will bring them into the land of Gilead and Lebanon, and place shall not be found for them. And he shall pass through the sea with affliction, and shall smite the waves in the sea, and all the deeps of the river shall dry up; and the pride of Assyria shall be brought down, and the scepter of Egypt shall depart. And I will strengthen them in the LORD; and they shall walk up and down in His name; saith the LORD."

INTRODUCTION to future events
Zechariah 9:1-14:21

The **DEFENSE** of Israel
Zechariah 9:1-10:12

The **DESCRIPTION** of the shepherds
Zechariah 11:1-17

1. The **RESULT** that will come –
   vv. 1-3

*"Open thy doors, O Lebanon, that the
fire may devour thy cedars. Howl, fir
tree; for the cedar is fallen, because the
mighty are spoiled; Howl, O ye oaks of
Bashan; for the forest of the vintage is
come down. There is a voice of the
howling of the shepherds; for their
glory is spoiled; a voice of the roaring
of young lions; for the pride of the
Jordan is spoiled."*

2. The **REJECTION** of the Good
   Shepherd – vv. 4-14

   (1) His **CONCERN** for His flock –
       vv. 4-7a

*"Thus saith the LORD, my God: Feed
the flock of the slaughter, Whose*

possessors slay them, and hold themselves not guilty; and they that sell them say, Blessed be the LORD; for I am rich; and their own shepherds pity them not. For I will no more pity the inhabitants of the land, saith the LORD, but, lo, I will deliver the men, every one, into his neighbor's hand, and into the hand of his king; and they shall smite the land, and out of their hand I will not deliver them. And I will feed the flock of slaughter, even you, O poor of the flock."

> **(2)** His <u>CALLING</u> of two poles – v. 7b (probably a shepherd's staff)

"And I took unto me two staves; the one I called Beauty, and the other I called Bands; and I fed the flock"

> **(3)** His <u>CUTTING OFF</u> of three shepherds – vv. 8-9

"Three shepherds also I cut off in one month; and my soul loathed them, and their soul also abhorred Me. Then said I, I will not feed you; that which dieth, let it die; and that which is to be cut off,

let it be cut off; and let the rest eat, every one, the flesh of another."

    (4)   His <u>COVENANT</u> that was broken – vv. 10-14

"And I took My staff, even Beauty, and cut it asunder, that I might break My covenant which I had made with all the peoples. And it was broken in that day; and so the poor of the flock that waited upon Me knew that it was the word of the LORD. And I said unto them, If ye think good, give me My price; and if not, forbear, So they weighed for My price thirty pieces of silver. And the LORD said unto me, Cast it unto the potter – a goodly price that I was prized at of them. And I took the thirty pieces of silver, and cast them to the potter in the house of the LORD. Then I cut asunder Mine other staff, even Bonds, that I might break the brotherhood between Judah and Israel."

    3. The <u>RISE</u> of the idol shepherd – vv. 15-17

"And the LORD said unto me, Take unto thee yet the instruments of a foolish shepherd; For, lo, I will raise up a shepherd in the land, who shall not visit those that are cut off, neither shall seek the young one, nor heal that which is broken, nor feed that which standeth still, but he shall eat the flesh of the fat, and tear their claws in pieces. Woe to the idol shepherd that leaveth the flock! The sword shall be upon his arm, and upon his right eye; his arm shall be clean dried up, and his right eye shall be utterly darkened.

The **DESTRUCTION** of the nations
Zechariah 12:1-14

    1. The **BURDEN** about Jerusalem – vv. 1-8

          (1)   The **SOURCE** of this burden – v. 1

"The burden of the word of the LORD for Israel, saith the LORD, Who stretcheth forth the heavens, and layeth the foundation of the earth, and formeth the spirit of man within him."

(2) The <u>SCOPE</u> of this
burden – v. 2a

"Behold, I will make Jerusalem a cup
of trembling unto all the people round
about..."

(3) The <u>SIEGE</u> against Israel
– v. 2b

"when they shall be in the siege both
against Judah and against Jerusalem"

(4) The <u>STONE</u> that will
affect all who come
against it – v. 3

"And in that day will I make Jerusalem
a burdensome stone for all peoples; all
that burden themselves with it shall be
cut in pieces, though all the people of
the earth be gathered together against
it."

(5) The <u>SMITING</u> of the
armies who come
against Jerusalem – v. 4

"In that day, saith the LORD, I will
smite every horse with astonishment,
and his rider with madness; and I will

open Mine eyes upon the house of Judah, and will smite every horse of the peoples with blindness."

> (6) The **STRENGTH** that the governors will manifest – vv. 5-6

"And the governors of Judah shall say in their heart, The inhabitants of Jerusalem shall be my strength in the LORD of hosts, their God. In that day will I make the governors of Judah like an hearth of fire among the wood, and like a torch of fire in a sheaf; and they shall devour all the peoples round about, on the right hand and on the left; and Jerusalem shall be inhabited again in her own place, even in Jerusalem."

> (7) The **SALVATION** of Judah – v. 7

"The LORD also shall save the tents of Judah first, that the glory of the house of David and the glory of the inhabitants of Jerusalem do magnify themselves against Judah."

(8) The SUPERNATURALNESS of the inhabitants of Jerusalem – v. 8

"In that day shall the LORD defend the inhabitants of Jerusalem; and he that is feeble among them at that day shall be like David: and the house of David shall be like God, like the Angel of the LORD before them."

2. The BATTLE that is coming – v. 9

"And it shall come to pass, in that day, that I will seek to destroy all the nations that come against Jerusalem."

3. The BLESSING of the Spirit – v. 10a

"And I will pour upon the house of David, and upon the inhabitants of Jerusalem, the Spirit of grace and of supplications..."

4. The BITTERNESS of Jewish believers – vv. 10b-14

"and they shall look upon Me Whom they have pierced, and they shall

mourn for Him, as one mourneth for his only son, and shall be in bitterness for his firstborn. In that day shall there be a great mourning in Jerusalem, as the mourning of Hadadrimmon, in the valley of Megiddon. And the land shall mourn, every family apart; the family of the house of David apart, and their wives apart; the family of the house of Nathan apart, and their wives apart; The family of the house of Levi apart, and their wives apart; the family of Shimei apart, and their wives apart; All the families that remain, every family apart, and their wives apart."

5. The <u>BENEFITS</u> of forgiveness – 13:1

"In that day there shall be a fountain opened to the house of David and to the inhabitants of Jerusalem for sin and for uncleanness."

The <u>DELIVERANCE</u> of God's people – Zechariah 13:2-9

1. From the <u>DECEPTION</u> of false prophets – vv. 2-6

"And it shall come to pass, in that day, saith the LORD of hosts, that I will cut off the names of the idols out of the land, and they shall no more be remembered, and also I will cause the prophets and the unclean spirit to pass out of the land. And it shall come to pass that, when any shall yet prophesy, then his father and his mother who begot him shall say unto him, Thou shalt not live; for thou speakest lies in the name of the LORD; and his father and his mother who begot him shall thrust him through when he prophesieth. And it shall come to pass, in that day, that the prophets shall be ashamed, every one, of his vision, when he hath prophesied; neither shall they wear a rough garment to deceive. But he shall say, I am no prophet, I am an husbandman; for man taught me to keep cattle from my youth. And one shall say unto him, What are these wounds in thine hands? Then he shall answer, Those with

which I was wounded in the house of my friends."

    2. Through the <u>DEATH</u> of the
       shepherd – v. 7a

"Awake, O sword, against my shepherd, and against the man who is my fellow, saith the LORD of hosts: smite the shepherd..."

<u>NOTE:</u> The usage of the pronoun *"MY shepherd"* and the words *"MY fellow"* and the usage of this passage in Matthew 26:41 and Mark 14:27 – and the connection with the *"piercing"* of Zechariah 12:10, and the frequent usage of the word *"shepherd"* to apply to our Lord – it appears that this is a Messianic reference and the *"smiting"* is caused by God.

    3. From the <u>DISPERSION</u> of the flock
       – v. 7b

"and the sheep shall be scattered; and I will turn Mine hand upon the little ones"

4. From the <u>DESTRUCTION</u> that is coming – vv. 8-9a

"And it shall come to pass, that in all the land, saith the LORD, two parts in it shall be cut off and die; but the third part shall be left in it. And I will bring the third part through the fire, and will refine them as silver is refined, and will try them as gold is tried..."

5. By their <u>DECISION</u> toward the LORD – v. 9b

"they shall call on My name, and I will hear them. I will say, It is My people; and they shall say, The LORD is my God."

THE <u>DESTINY</u> OF THE NATIONS
Zechariah 14:1-21

1. The <u>COMING</u> of the Day of the LORD – 14:1-8

   (1) The <u>GATHERING</u> of all nations – vv. 1-2

"Behold, the day of the LORD cometh, and thy spoil shall be divided in the midst of thee. For I will gather all nations against Jerusalem to battle; and the city shall be taken, and the houses rifled, and the women ravished; and half of the city shall go forth into captivity, and the residue of the people shall not be cut off from the city."

(2) The <u>GUARANTEE</u> of the LORD – v. 3

"Then shall the LORD go forth, and fight against those nations, as when He fought in the day of battle."

(3) The <u>GROUND</u> upon which He will stand – vv. 4-7

"And His feet shall stand in that day upon the Mount of Olives, which is before Jerusalem on the east, and the Mount of Olives shall cleave in its midst toward the east and toward the west, and there shall be a very great valley; and half of the mountain shall remove toward the north, and half of it toward the south. And ye shall flee to the valley of the mountains; for the

valley of the mountains shall reach unto Azel; yea, ye shall flee, as ye fled from before the earthquake in the days of Uzziah, king of Judah; and the LORD, my God, shall come, and all the saints with thee. And it shall come to pass, in that day, that the light shall not be clear, nor dark, But it shall be one day which shall be known to the LORD, not day, nor night; but it shall come to pass that, at evening time, it shall be light."

(4) The GOING OUT of living waters– v. 8

"And it shall be, in that day, that living waters shall go out from Jerusalem; half of them toward the former sea, and half of them toward the western sea; in summer and in winter shall it be."

2. The CROWNING of the Lord as KING – vv. 9-11

"And the LORD shall be king over all the earth; in that day shall there be one LORD, and His Name one. All the land shall be turned like a plain from Geba

to Rimmon south of Jerusalem; and it
shall be lifted up, and inhabited in its
place, from Benjamin's gate unto the
place of the first gate, unto the corner
gate, and from the tower of Hananel
unto the king's winepresses. And men
shall dwell in it, and there shall be no
more utter destruction; but Jerusalem
shall be safely inhabited."

3. The <u>CONSEQUENCES</u> upon the
   nations – vv. 12-15

"And this shall be the plague with
which the LORD will smite all the
peoples that have fought against
Jerusalem: their flesh shall consume
away while they stand upon their feet,
and their eyes shall consume away in
their holes, and their tongue shall
consume away in their mouth. And it
shall come to pass, in that day, that a
great tumult from the LORD shall be
among them; and they shall lay hold
every one on the hand of his neighbor,
and his hand shall rise up against the
hand of his neighbor. And Judah also
shall fight at Jerusalem; and the
wealth of all the heathen round about

shall be gathered together – gold, and silver, and apparel – in great abundance. And so shall be the plague of the horse, of the mule, of the camel, and of the ass, and of all the beasts that shall be in these tents, as this plague."

4. The <u>CHARACTER</u> of the coming Kingdom – vv. 16-21

"And it shall come to pass that every one that is left of all the nations which came against Jerusalem shall even go up from year to year to worship the King, the LORD of hosts, and to keep the feast of tabernacles. And it shall be that whoever will not come up of all the families of the earth unto Jerusalem to worship the King, the LORD of hosts, even upon them shall be no rain. And if the family of Egypt go not up, and come not, that have no rain, there shall be the plague, with which the LORD shall smite the heathen that come not up to keep the feast of tabernacles. This shall be the punishment of Egypt, and the punishment of all nations that come not up to keep the feast of tabernacles. In that day shall there be

upon the bells of the horses, HOLINESS UNTO THE LORD; and the pots in the LORD's house shall be like the bowls before the altar. Yea, every pot in Jerusalem and in Judah shall be holiness unto the LORD of hosts; and all they that sacrifice shall come and take of them, and seethe in them; and in that day there shall be no more a Canaanite in the house of the LORD of hosts."

MALACHI
Malachi 1:1-4:6

INTRODUCTION
Malachi 1:1

"The burden of the word of the LORD to Israel by Malachi"

The meaning of his name – *"My messenger"* or *"the messenger of the LORD"*

There are 27 questions in the book, and the term *"the LORD of hosts"* is used 24 times, and the most remarkable fact about this book of four chapters, is the usage of the tetragrammaton – the sacred name of the LORD – "YAHVEH" – it appears 55 times!

THE **PRIORITY** OF GOD'S LOVE – Malachi 1:1-5

"The burden of the word of the LORD to Israel by Malachi. I have loved you, saith the LORD. Yet ye say, Wherein hast Thou loved us? Was not Esau Jacob's brother? Saith the LORD; yet I

loved Jacob, and I hated Esau, and laid his mountains and his heritage waste for the dragons of the wilderness, whereas Edom saith, We are impoverished, but we will return and build the desolate places, thus saith the LORD of hosts, They shall build, but I will throw down; and they shall call them, The border of wickedness, and, The people against whom the LORD hath indignation forever. And your eyes shall see, and ye shall say, The LORD will be magnified from the border of Israel."

1. The <u>DECLARATION</u> comes from the mouth of the LORD Himself! v. 2a – *"I have loved you, saith the LORD"*

Isaiah 43:4 – *"Since thou wast precious in My sight, thou hast been honorable, and I have loved thee; therefore will I give men for thee, and people for thy life."*

2. The <u>DOUBT</u> was in the hearts of the people – v. 2b – *"Wherein hast Thou loved us?"*

3. The <u>DECISION</u> to choose Jacob over Esau was based on God's sovereignty – v. 2c – *"Was not Esau Jacob's brother? Saith the LORD; yet I loved Jacob."*

4. The <u>DESOLATION</u> of Edom was clear evidence that God had chosen Jacob and rejected Esau – v. 3 – *"and I hated Esau"*

5. The <u>DETERMINATION</u> of Edom to rebuild would not be successful! – v. 4a – *"Whereas Edom saith, We are impoverished, but we will return and build the desolate places..."*

6. The <u>DESTINY</u> of Edom was clear – v. 4b – *"thus saith the LORD of hosts, They shall build, but I will throw down; and they shall call them, The border of wickedness, and, The people against whom the LORD hath indignation forever."*

7. The <u>DEMONSTRATION</u> of God's love would spread outside of the land of Israel – v. 5 – *"and your eyes shall see, and ye shall say,*

The LORD be magnified from the border of Israel."

THE **POLLUTION** OF GOD'S LOVE
Malachi 1:6-14

1. The <u>COMPARISONS</u> that reveal their lack of respect – v. 6a

   (1) Son to a father – *"Where is Mine honor?"*

   (2) Servant to a Master – *"Where is My fear?"*

2. The <u>CONFRONTATION</u> of the priests – v. 6b – *"that despise My Name"*

3. The <u>CONTEMPT</u> they reveal for true worship – vv. 7-8a

"Ye offer polluted bread upon Mine altar; and ye say, Wherein have we polluted Thee? In that ye say, The table of the LORD is contemptible. And if ye offer the blind for sacrifice, is it not evil? And if ye offer the lame and sick, is it not evil?"

4. The <u>CHALLENGE</u> to their attitudes – v. 8b – *"Offer it now unto thy governor; will he be pleased with thee, or accept thy person? Saith the LORD of hosts."*

5. The <u>CALLING</u> upon God that is needed – v. 9

"And now, I pray you, beseech God that He will be gracious unto us. This hath been by your means; will He regard your persons? Saith the LORD of hosts."

6. The <u>CONDEMNATION</u> of their worship – v. 10

"Who is there even among you that would shut the doors for nought? Neither do ye kindle fire on Mine altar for nought. I have no pleasure in you, saith the LORD of hosts, neither will I accept an offering at your hand."

7. The <u>CHARACTER</u> of God requires obedience and the future will prove it – v. 11

"For from the rising of the sun even unto the going down of the same, My name shall be great among the Gentiles, and in every place incense shall be offered unto My name, and a pure offering; for My name shall be great among the heathen, saith the LORD of hosts."

8. Their <u>COMMENTS</u> about worship will not be tolerated – vv. 12-13

"But ye have profaned it, in that ye say, The table of the LORD is polluted; and the fruit of it, even its meat, is contemptible. Ye said also, Behold, what a weariness is it! And ye have snuffed at it, saith the LORD of hosts; and ye brought that which was torn, and the lame, and the sick; thus ye brought an offering. Should I accept this of your hand? Saith the LORD.

9. The <u>CURSE</u> that will result – v. 14

"But cursed be the deceiver, who hath in his flock a male, and voweth, and sacrificeth unto the Lord a corrupt thing; for I am a great King, saith the

LORD of hosts, and My name is dreadful among the heathen."

THE **PUNISHMENT** OF GOD'S LOVE – Malachi 2:1-10

1. The **PEOPLE** who are being addressed – v. 1 – *"And now, O ye priests, this commandment is for you"*

2. The **PURPOSE** of their lives and ministries was being ignored and neglected – v. 2a – *"If ye will not hear, and if ye will not lay it to heart, to give glory unto My Name, saith the LORD of hosts..."*

3. The **PUNISHMENT** would be a *"curse"* sent from God – vv. 2b-3

"I will even send a curse upon you, and I will curse your blessings; yea, I have cursed them already, because ye do not lay it to heart. Behold, I will corrupt your seed, and spread dung upon your faces, even the dung of your solemn feasts; and one shall take you away with it."

4. The <u>PLACE</u> of God's covenant with Levi would be clear – v. 4

"And ye shall know that I have sent this commandment unto you, that My covenant might be with Levi, saith the LORD of hosts."

5. The <u>PRINCIPLES</u> upon which a godly priesthood should be built – vv. 5-7

"My covenant was with him of life and peace; and I gave them to him for the fear with which he feared Me, and was afraid before My name. The law of truth was in his mouth, and iniquity was not found in his lips; he walked with Me in peace and equity, and did turn any away from iniquity. For the priest's lips should keep knowledge, and they should seek the law at his mouth; for he is the messenger of the LORD of hosts."

6. The <u>PROBLEMS</u> that developed among the priests of that day – v. 8

"But ye are departed out of the way; ye have cause many to stumble at the law;

ye have corrupted the covenant of Levi, saith the LORD of hosts."

7. The **PLAN** which God will now use in dealing with these priests – v. 9

"Therefore have I also made you contemptible and base before all the people, according as ye have not kept My ways, but have been partial in the law."

THE **PRACTICE** OF GOD'S LOVE
Malachi 2:10-17

1. Their **RELATIONSHIP** to God should have stopped them – v. 10a
    "Have we not all one father?"

2. Their **RECOGNITION** of creation should have prevented what they did – v. 10b – *"Hath not one God created us?"*

3. Their **RESPONSE** to the covenant does not make send – v. 10c – *"Why do we deal treacherously every man against his brother, by profaning the covenant of our fathers?"*

4. The <u>REALITY</u> of what they had done – v. 11

"Judah hath dealt treacherously, and an abomination is committed in Israel and in Jerusalem; for Judah hath profaned the holiness of the LORD which He loved, and hath married the daughter of a strange god."

5. The <u>RESULT</u> that God will bring – v. 12

"The LORD will cut off the man that doeth this, the master and the scholar, out of the tabernacles of Jacob, and him that offereth an offering unto the LORD of hosts."

6. Their <u>REACTIONS</u> would not convince the LORD – v. 13

"And this have ye done again, covering the altar of the LORD with tears, with weeping, and with crying out, insomuch that He regardeth not an offering any more, or receiveth it with good will at your hand."

7. Their <u>REALIZATION</u> of what they had done – vv.14-15a

"Yet ye say, Wherefore? Because the LORD hath been witness between thee and the wife of thy youth, against whom thou hast dealt treacherously; yet is she thy companion, and the wife of thy covenant? And did not he make one? Yet had he the residue of the spirit. And wherefore one? That he might seek a godly seed."

8. The <u>REPENTANCE</u> that was needed – vv. 15b-16

"Therefore, take heed to your spirit, and let none deal treacherously against the wife of his youth. For the LORD, the God of Israel, saith that He hateth putting away, for one covereth violence with his garment, saith the LORD of hosts; therefore, take heed to your spirit, that ye deal not treacherously."

9. Their <u>REASONING</u> did not impress the LORD – v. 17

"Ye have wearied the LORD with your words. Yet ye say, Wherein have we wearied Him? When ye say, Every one that doeth evil is good in the sight of the LORD, and He delighteth in them; or Where is the God of judgment?"

THE **PURITY** OF GOD'S LOVE
Malachi 3:1-6

1. The <u>COMING</u> of God's messenger – 3:1

"Behold, I will send My messenger, and he shall prepare the way before Me; and the Lord, Whom ye seek, shall suddenly come to His temple, even the Messenger of the covenant, Whom ye delight in; behold, He shall come, saith the LORD of hosts."

2. The <u>CLEANSING</u> which He will bring – vv. 2-3

"But who may abide the day of His coming? And who shall stand when He appeareth? For He is like a refiner and purifier of silver; and He shall purify the sons of Levi, and purge them like gold and silver, that they may offer

unto the LORD an offering in
righteousness."

   3. The <u>CONSEQUENCE</u> that will take
      place after the refining is done –
      v. 4

"Then shall the offering of Judah and
Jerusalem be pleasant unto the LORD,
as in the days of old, and as in former
years."

   4. The <u>CONDEMNATION</u> of the
      Lord's judgment – v. 5

"And I will come near to you to
judgment; and I will be a swift witness
against the sorcerers, and against the
adulterers, and against false swearers,
and against those that oppress the
hireling in his wagers, the widow, and
the fatherless, and that turn aside the
stranger from his right, and fear not
Me, saith the LORD of hosts."

   5. The <u>CHANGELESSNESS</u> of the
      LORD – v. 6a

"For I am the LORD, I change not."

6. The <u>CONSUMING</u> that will NOT take place – v. 6b

"therefore ye sons of Jacob are not consumed"

THE <u>PLEA</u> OF GOD'S LOVE
Malachi 3:7-12

1. The <u>CONDITION</u> of the people was the problem – v. 7a

"Even from the days of your fathers ye are gone away from Mine ordinances, and have not kept them,

The <u>CALL</u> to return to the LORD is where repentance begins – v. 7b

"Return unto Me, and I will return unto you, saith the LORD of hosts"

2. The <u>CONCERN</u> of the people shows how easily we can ignore and neglect our spiritual responsibilities – v. 7c

"But ye said, Wherein shall we return?"

3. The <u>CONDEMNATION</u> of the LORD was not anticipated – v. 8

"Will a man rob God? Yet ye have robbed Me. But ye say, Wherein have we robbed Thee? In tithes and offerings."

4. The <u>CURSE</u> that was the result – v. 9

"Ye are cursed with a curse; for ye have robbed Me, even this whole nation."

5. The <u>COMMITMENT</u> that was now needed to remove the curse - v. 10a

"Bring all the tithes into the storehouse, that there may be meat in Mine house."

6. The <u>CONSEQUENCES</u> which they can expect if they respond - vv. 10b-12

"and prove Me now herewith, saith the LORD of hosts, if I will not open for you the windows of heaven, and pour out for you a blessing, that there shall not

be room enough to receive it. And I will rebuke the devourer for your sakes, and he shall not destroy the fruits of your ground; neither shall your vine cast its fruit before the time in the field, saith the LORD of hosts. And all nations shall call you blessed; for ye shall be a delightsome land, saith the LORD of hosts."

THE **PROFIT** OF GOD'S LOVE
Malachi 3:13-18

1. The <u>REBUKE</u> of the LORD – v. 13a

"Your words have been stout against me, saith the LORD."

2. The <u>REACTION</u> they had to the LORD's rebuke – v. 13b

"Yet ye say, What have we spoken, so much against Thee?"

3. The <u>REASONING</u> they had was an attack upon the LORD Himself – v. 14

"Ye have said, It is vain to serve God; and what profit is it that we have kept

His ordinance, and that we have walked mournfully before the LORD of hosts?"

    4. The <u>RESULTS</u> they desired were seen in the lives of the ungodly – v. 15

"And now we call the proud happy; yea, they that work wickedness are set up; yea, they that tempt God are even delivered."

    5. The <u>RESPONSE</u> of the godly – v. 16a

"Then they that feared the LORD spoke often one to another; and the LORD hearkened and heard it."

    6. The <u>REMEMBRANCE</u> of the godly – v. 16b

"a book of remembrance was written before Him for them that feared the LORD, and that thought upon His Name."

    7. The <u>REASSURANCE</u> of the LORD to those who honor Him – v. 17

"And they shall be Mine, saith the LORD of hosts, in that day when I make up My jewels; and I will spare them, as a man spareth his own son that serveth him."

8. Their <u>RETURN</u> will reveal the truth as to the profit in serving the LORD – v. 18

"Then shall ye return, and discern between the righteous and the wicked, between him that serveth God, and him that serveth Him not."

THE <u>POWER</u> OF GOD'S LOVE
Malachi 4:1-6

1. The <u>CONSEQUENCES</u> for the wicked – 4:1

"For, behold, the day cometh, that shall burn like an oven, and all the proud, yea, and all that do wickedly, shall be stubble; and the day that cometh shall burn them up, saith the LORD of hosts, that it shall leave them neither root nor branch."

2. The <u>CHARACTER</u> of the Messiah –
   v. 2

*"But unto you that fear My Name shall
the Sun of righteousness arise with
healing in His wings; and ye shall go
forth, and grow up like calves of the
stall."*

3. The <u>CONQUEST</u> of the righteous –
   v. 3

*"And ye shall tread down the wicked;
for they shall be ashes under the soles
of your feet in the day that I shall do
this, saith the LORD of hosts."*

4. The <u>CHARGE</u> to remember – v. 4

*"Remember the law of Moses, My
servant, which I commanded unto him
in Horeb for all Israel, with the
statutes and judgments."*

5. The <u>COMING</u> of Elijah – vv. 5-6

*"Behold, I send you Elijah, the prophet,
before the coming of the great and
dreadful day of the LORD; And he shall
turn the heart of the fathers to the
children, and the heart of the children*

to their fathers, lest I come and smite the earth with a curse."